ROYAL NAVY DESTROYERS

1893 TO THE PRESENT DAY

MAURICE COCKER FRINA

The
History
Press

HMS *Bristol*, Type 82, showing complex superstructure. (MoD (Navy))

First published in 1981, this edition 2011

The History Press
The Mill, Brimscombe Port
Stroud, Gloucestershire, GL5 2QG
www.thehistorypress.co.uk

British Library Cataloguing in Publication Data.
A catalogue record for this book is available from the British Library.

ISBN 978 0 7524 6159 5

Typesetting and origination by The History Press
Printed in Great Britain
Manufacturing managed by Jellyfish Print Solutions Ltd

ROYAL NAVY DESTROYERS

Contents

Type 45 destroyer HMS *Daring*. (BAE Systems)

Foreword

BY

CAPTAIN DAVID HART DYKE CBE LVO ROYAL NAVY

This is a fascinating history of the destroyer in the Royal Navy which begins at the end of the nineteenth century. With the invention of the torpedo came the development of ships to deliver the weapon and to counter the new threat. First came the small craft called torpedo boats and torpedo catchers, followed by the larger and faster torpedo boat destroyers. HMS *Havock* of 260 tons was the first of this later type completed in 1893. Thus evolved many classes of ships, known simply as destroyers, which exist in the Fleet today and in many other navies, though they are no longer specialised in a single role.

Since the Second World War, the roles of the destroyer and frigate have gradually merged, both having more of an all-round capability to deal with threats from below or above the water. However, up until the early 1960s the destroyer's main armament was guns and the frigate was primarily equipped for anti-submarine warfare. The advent of the ship-borne helicopter – with the ability to launch both torpedoes and anti-ship missiles – did much to enhance the versatility of the destroyer and frigate, giving them comparable capabilities.

My thirty years in the Navy saw the open-bridge all-gun destroyer develop into the multi-role vessel with more missiles than guns: such was HMS *Coventry*, a Type 42 destroyer, which was the first ship in Royal Navy history to fire missiles in anger in 1982.

I venture to suggest that the highly sophisticated destroyer as a class of ship will continue in the Royal Navy in the future, though in much smaller numbers than the frigate, which will remain the 'maid of all work'.

Preface

The purpose of this book is to fill a gap in existing naval literature by being the first work to trace the history of the destroyer from its inception as a 'torpedo boat destroyer' to the guided missile versions of the modern RN. Each destroyer is described as it was accepted into service from the shipyard and, unless particularly noteworthy, later alterations and modernisations are omitted because of their number. Among the appendices are lists of the causes of loss of those destroyers sunk in the two world wars.

The destroyer has become a thing of the past now, for the current guided missile destroyers have little in common with the vessels of previous decades. Instead, the frigate, evolved during the Second World War, is increasing in numbers, size and firepower. Therefore, I would dedicate this book to those vessels which may soon be just a memory – to the destroyers of the Royal Navy and all those who sailed in them.

M.P. Cocker
Cleveleys, Lancashire

Left: HMS *Cardiff*, 'Towns' class, launching. Compare this photograph with HMS *Atherstone* for difference in shape of hull and superstructure. (Vickers) **Below**: HMS *Defender*, 'D' class, off Walney Island. (Vickers)

Acknowledgements

I wish to mention with grateful thanks the assistance and help which I have received from many sources amongst whom must be mentioned the following official organisations and individuals:

Admiralty Departments (descriptions as in 1961), now Ministry of Defence (Navy): Department of the Chief of Naval Information; Material Branch I and Material Branch II; Admiralty Librarian and Staff; Ministry of Defence, Director of Public Relations (Navy) (Cdr F.E.R. Phillips, RN, Lt R.V.S. Neilson, RN); Office Services (Editing) (F.S. White, Esq.); Historical Branch (J.D. Brown Esq., Miss M.W. Thirkettle); The Fleet Air Arm Museum (the Curator, Lt-Cdr L.A. Cox, RN, and staff); Vickers Shipbuilding Group, Barrow-in-Furness (D.W. Robinson, Esq., Press and Public Relations Officer); Cammell Laird Shipbuilders Ltd (W.K. Fox, Esq., Assistant Manager-Information Services); The Royal Institution of Naval Architects (J. Rosewarn, Esq., Assistant Secretary (Administration) for permission to use material by the late Sir A.J. Sims from his paper 'Warships 1860-1960'); Real Photographs Ltd; Nashua Copycat Ltd; Sampson Low, Marston & Co. Ltd, for permission to use losses statistics from *Ships of the Royal Navy*, statement of losses during the Second World War, 3 September 1939–2 September 1945, HMSO 1947, also Amendment No.1 to the above, HMSO 1949; Imperial War Museum, Department of Photographs (Mrs L. Willmot, E. Hine, J. Harding and M. Willis, Esq.); Swan Hunter Shipbuilders Ltd, Hebburn Shipyard (K.G. Burdis, Esq.); J. Wilkinson, Esq., for photographs of the damaged HMS *Saumarez* and HMS *Volage*; Vickers Ltd, Millbank, London (M.J. Barry, Esq.); Cath Thurgood, BAE Systems.

I am also grateful to Pauline for typing portions of the first edition and additionally being helpful and full of suggestions. If by neglect on my part I have omitted any person or organisation then I trust that my apologies will be accepted.

This author contributes to the Friends Funds of the Imperial War Museum, the National Maritime Museum and the Merseyside Maritime Museum.

Abbreviations

'A' Bracket	A metal bracket proud of the underwater hull holding the outer propeller shaft rigid	mm	Millimetre
		MoD(N)	Ministry of Defence (Navy)
		MTB	Motor Torpedo Boat
AA	Anti-aircraft	mtg	Mounting
AS	Anti-submarine	M/V	Motor Vessel
Calibre	The diameter of a projectile, e.g. 4.7in, 21in	nm	Nautical mile
		pdr	Pounder
CP	Central pivot (a gun mounting)	P No.	Pennant (Pendant) number
DCT	Director Control Tower	posn	Position
Displacement	The quantity of water in tons displaced by a ship	pp	Length between perpendiculars
		QF	Quick firing
DP	Dual purpose	RAN	Royal Australian Navy
E-Boat	A light tonnage (fast patrol boat) enemy surface craft	RAS	Replenishment at sea
		RCN	Royal Canadian Navy
Full-load	The displacement tonnage of a warship plus the weight of ammunition, fuel and stores	RDF	Radio Direction Finding
		RHN	Royal Hellenic Navy
		RNN	Royal Netherlands Navy
HA	High angle	R/T	Radio Telephony
HIMS	His Imperial Majesty's Ship (Japan)	shp	Shaft horse power
HMAS	His Majesty's Australian Ship	SS	Steam ship
HMCS	His Majesty's Canadian Ship	TB	Torpedo Boat
HMS	His/Her Majesty's Ship	TBD	Torpedo Boat Destroyer
hp	Horse power	TC	Torpedo Catcher
HSMS	High Speed Minesweeping	TD	Torpedo Destroyer
ihp	Indicated horse power	TT(s)	Torpedo tube(s)
Is	Island/s	U-boat	Any enemy submarine
LA	Low angle	wl	Water line (length on)
L(oa)	Length overall	W/T	Wireless Telegraphy
MG	Machine gun	YD	Yard (for shipbuilding yard)

Notes

GUNSHIELDS

In early classes, the gun was generally mounted upon a prepared deck base or platform and surrounded by canvas dodgers but, these being obstructive, a small plate shield of three sides and top was mounted over the gun breech and dropped to the line of the recoil barrel. Later shield designs were more elongated and extended to within a few inches of deck level. Later still the shield extended further back until all that was needed was a back plate and the turret was completed as in the 'Lightning' class.

LEADERS AND CLASSES

Between the wars, classes were built in eights with a specially designed leader to bring the class to nine (example 'H' class 1936). During 1939–45, the classes were built in eights and one of this number was selected to be leader (example 'S' class 1942).

PENNANT LETTERS AND NUMBERS

Originally numbers were given on naval stations and ships changed their numbers on passing from one station to another. About 1910 the Admiralty took the matter in hand and compiled a Naval Pennant List. Ships were grouped under the distinguishing flag of the type – TBs under the Red Burgee, destroyers under the Flag Superior H, and so on. Ships with nucleus crews in the 2nd or 3rd Fleets had a distinguishing letter to indicate the manning port, D – Devonport, N – Nore, P – Portsmouth. This ceased during the First World War. At the start of the Second World there were more destroyers than could be accommodated under one flag superior, and they were numbered D00 to D99, F00 to F99 and H00 to H99.

This list in use today, D for destroyers, F for frigates, is published in *Jane's Fighting Ships* with which most readers will no doubt be familiar.

NOMENCLATURE – DESCRIPTIVE TITLE

The naming of HM Ships and the type of ship is no part of the subject of this book, but it will be noted that after the torpedo boats were constructed, the vessels to counter the torpedo boats were described as torpedo catchers, torpedo destroyers, and even torpedo gun boats, none of these titles being in the writer's mind truly descriptive; therefore, the term torpedo catcher in this book refers to all ships designed to counter the torpedo boat prior to the advent of the torpedo boat destroyer. It is difficult to ascertain exactly when the name 'Destroyer' came into common usage as the term TBD was retained even in the Navy List until 1919. As early as June 1906 it was shortened to Destroyer when referring to Destroyer Flotillas, as opposed to individual ships. No one Admiralty fleet order lays down that one term or the other should be used but again in 1917, an order refers to 'TBD's' and a further order in 1919 refers to 'Destroyers'.

SPELLING

During the First World War the spelling of GHURKA, KHANDAHAR and KHARTOUM included an H as the second letter. During the Second World War the H was mostly dropped, i.e. GURKA, KARTOUM and KANDAHAR. This change was adopted for unknown reasons.

Introduction

One of the many species of fish which abound in the oceans of the world is the 'Torpedo', otherwise known as the ray or electric ray, and the purpose of its inherent electricity is to disable, halt and immobilise the other fish which are its neighbours and prey. Perhaps therefore it is fitting that an underwater weapon now so well known and extremely effective should have been named thus more than a century ago.

In fact what we know as mines were also identified as torpedoes and the theory of underwater destruction of the enemy's vessels was appreciated as early as 1850. Very little progress, however, had been made towards making the torpedo into a self-propelled destruction charge, and it was not until the year 1866 that the English manager of an Italian engineering firm invented the true torpedo which is still the same in its essential principles as when Robert Whitehead first successfully completed his trials of the 'Hydrostatic Torpedo'.

Four years later, the Admiralty commended the weapon to Parliament and the manufacturing rights were purchased for the sum of £15,000. In 1877, HMS *Shah* unsuccessfully attempted to torpedo a Peruvian naval vessel *Huascar* with which she was engaged in conflict.

The problem the Admiralty had now to face was how best to employ the new weapon. It was, as most agreed, a weapon of surprise and stealth and indeed at that time, with a speed of 6 knots, the odds were in favour of the attacked vessel escaping the somewhat erratic course of the torpedo which had a limited range of about 4 cables. Therefore, attacks during the dark hours or in poor visibility were more favoured and carried out by the ship's launch with a torpedo slung on either beam and released at the appropriate moment.

It then became evident, that, as the torpedo improved, the ships of the fleet of the time were not of sufficient speed to approach within torpedo range and retire without seriously exposing themselves to the enemy's gunfire. Therefore a small but comparatively speedy craft was designed and produced in some numbers, for just a foray, although the ships of the fleet retained their torpedo tubes (this being the approved mode of launching from large vessels), just in case they, too, might be sufficiently close to bring their new weapons to bear. The first torpedo boat, although built by Thornycroft, was ordered by the Norwegian government in 1873 with a length of 57ft, displacement of 7.5 tons and a speed of 15kts (on trials), but in 1877 HMS *Lightning* became the first Royal Naval torpedo boat with 19kts on the measured mile. Thereafter this type of vessel grew in size and numbers with the speed increasing steadily with power, and a typical torpedo boat of 1886 by White made 20kts on 1,100shp, displaced 125 tons and carried three 14in tubes. So the evolution continued, for now it was evident that a host of such craft would well be a menace to any fleet.

As a remedy, a second type of small craft known as the 'torpedo catcher' was designed. The first for the Royal Navy was HMS *Rattlesnake* from Lairds in 1886, but they failed to live up to expectations, possibly because they displaced 400-800 tons and were of insufficient speed to bring the torpedo boats to bay (see Appendix 3).

The next design type was named the 'torpedo boat destroyer' and, although a change of policy for the Admiralty, in destroying (or trying to) their own creation, it was initially successful, and when the need for seaworthiness rather than excessive speed was realised, then the destroyer design (as it was known) forged ahead and ousted the very craft it was to destroy. HMS *Havock* was the first destroyer to be commissioned and came from the Yarrow yards in 1893. It had two shafts driven by triple expansion engines and made

HMS *Mentor*, Hawthorn 'M' class, flying both the Red and White Ensigns. (Swan Hunter)

27kts. About sixty of these torpedo boat destroyers (or TBDs as they were known) were built to Admiralty specifications between 1893 and 1900, with slight improvements and modifications by the builders who had had a very free hand in the design. These formed the 'A' and 'B' classes.

By now the turbine had made its effect on the Admiralty by the appearance of the Turbinia at the 1897 Spithead Review, and in 1899 HMS *Viper*, a vessel of 312 tons, made 37.1kts at 12,000ihp on trials. HMS *Viper* had a formidable armament for a ship of 210ft: one 12-pounder, five 6-pounder guns and two 18in torpedo tubes. A similar boat to the *Viper* was HMS *Cobra* which had been completed by Armstrong-Whitworth (Tyne) but only had a short service career as she broke in two in 1901. Just over a month later HMS *Viper* was also lost, being wrecked on Alderney. After the *Cobra* and *Viper* losses, snake names were not repeated, although HMS *Rattlesnake* saw much service and was sold in 1921.

The trouble appeared to be that the long narrow-beamed hulls were under great stress with the tremendous power of the turbines and hard driving into short seas. When the destroyers grew beamier, then their seaworthiness improved.

The 'C' class was of no particular advance upon the earlier classes, and the boats were apparently constructed proportionately between four or five yards to Admiralty specifications, but the builders own designs. HMS *Velox* of this class had triple expansion engines for cruising although she relied on turbines for her main propulsive power.

The 'D' class followed – smaller and handier vessels and all to one design. Their appearance was improved for they each had two funnels and turtle-back bows, the only differences being that four of them had outboard rudders. To continue in chronological order of entering service, HMS *Taku* was accepted into service from another source, and this is the proper place to mention that the Royal Navy received excellent service from ex-Chilean, Turkish, Portuguese and Greek destroyers during the First World War; and ex-Brazilian, French and Turkish vessels during the Second World War; nor must we forget the 'Destroyers for Bases' which were as valuable in 1940. The majority of the 'ex' destroyers were new buildings, but a number were purchased outright or leased.

In 1907, HMS *Swift* was commissioned; she was a vessel far ahead of her time, not approached for size and power in destroyer-building until 1937, some thirty years later.

A note must now be made regarding the formation of the destroyer class system. The 'A', 'B', 'C', 'D', 'E', 'F', 'G', 'H' and 'I' classes did not exist as such until 1913 when the Admiralty enquired into the then existing method and system of destroyer names and naming and decided to introduce some uniformity by grouping all the existing 27kt ships of the 1890s into the 'A' class, and the 30kt boats which followed would form the 'B' class, and so forth to the 'K' class. The class to follow after 'K' would be 'L', and would have names commencing with that letter and all following classes would conform to the new ruling. The system worked well even though such a large class as the Admiralty 'M' had, due to its size, four initial letters allotted to it. Further large classes were the Admiralty 'R', 'S', 'V' and 'W', the 'R' class having three letters and the 'S' two. No 'J' class was formed until the 'Javelins' during the late 1930s. Two systematically named groups of boats were however the 'E-River' and the 'F-Tribal' classes of 1903–06.

The 'F' class were reasonably beamy ships with good speed, and the 'G' class were slightly larger but slower, notable for being the first destroyers to mount the 4in gun.

With the 'H' and 'I' classes, there was little overall change, although both mounted the 4in gun, there being two in the 'H' and 'I' boats and three in the 'K' class which had increased tonnage and speed on two or three shafts according to the builders' variations.

At the 'L' class, standardisation in build was virtually complete although the boats had either two or three funnels.

Increased tonnage again with armament and tubes were features of the Admiralty 'M' class (which also attained a record number of names to the class, there being a total of eighty-five), and high speed was maintained although on three shafts.

Not unnaturally, the 'big three' destroyer constructors (Yarrow, Thornycroft and Hawthorn) supplied a small number of their own modified design vessels of most Admiralty classes, and they had also a little advantage in speed.

Two classes then followed composed completely of leaders, being ships which were of 1,500 tons and exceeding 320ft in length. These were the 'Marksman' and 'Anzac' classes of 1915–16.

In 1916, a virtual repeat of the Admiralty 'M' class was decided upon and in that year the first of the Admiralty 'R' class was completed. Ships of this class had more speed although only on two shafts, but all

HMS *Lightning* on builder's trials on the Thames, 1877. (Vosper Thornycroft)

The earliest torpedo boats, 1878. (IWM)

had geared turbines. The following large class in 1918 was called the Admiralty 'S' class, and maintained the previous standard of the 'R' class together with a larger bridge. HMS *Shikari* (which much later on had the distinction of being the first destroyer in the Royal Navy to have radar, albeit for evaluation) of this class was not completed until 1924, nor HMS *Thracian* till 1922.

Then followed what is probably the most famous class of all, the Admiralty 'V' class which became identified with the follow-up class, the Admiralty 'W' to form the 'V' and 'W' classes of both world wars. They were fine ships, to realistic designs and with perhaps the most significant step forward in gunnery mounting in that the guns were superimposed in the now familiar positions of A, B, X and Y.

With peace in late 1918, two further leader classes were under construction, being being the Thornycroft type and the Admiralty large design, and, apart from the fourteen ships of the Admiralty modified 'W' class, were the first destroyers to mount the 4.7in gun.

Destroyer building slowed up tremendously and thirty-eight ships of the last mentioned class were cancelled. In 1924, however, the Admiralty asked Yarrow and Thornycroft to design and construct one destroyer each to embody all the lessons of the past thirty-one years and First World War. The two ships were known as the Experimental 'A' class, and these two destroyers were the prototypes of the long line of classes to be built in alphabetical sequence from the 'A' of 1929 to the 'Zambesi' school of 1944. They had greater endurance, and gunnery control, which really commenced with the 'V' and 'W', reached its greatest height in 1944 with the 'Later Battle' class which carried an American pattern of director tower. Further equipment fitted at intervals was really effective W/T and R/T with Asdic radar and other electronic devices of war.

Then followed the new 'A' class of 1929, and a destroyer of this class displaced about 1,400 tons and made over 35kts at 34,000shp. The armament in the main consisted of 4.7in guns with lighter weapons such as 2-pounders and machine guns. The 'A' to 'Intrepid' classes were, with modification, of like build and design.

Mention must however be made of a one-design class in 1929, this ship being HMS *Codrington* which, for her period, was all that was best in destroyer design. It should be noted also that since the Admiralty 'S' class of 1918, all destroyers were twin-funnelled and had two pole masts with yardarms.

In 1937, however, a new concept in destroyer design was evolved which completely altered the outward appearance of this type of ship. These ships were named after tribes and suffered 50 per cent losses during the Second World War. The 'Tribal' class, as it was known, had a main armament of eight 4.7in guns in twin shields, mounted in the now familiar A, B, X and Y positions. This splendid design was followed by the 'Javelin' class which comprised three groups of eight ships, each of which had names commencing with either a J, K or N; the full class comprised twenty-four ships with eight to each of the letters.

Following was the 'Lightning' class with two groups of eight ships which had names commencing with either an L or M, and all were one-funnelled (as were the two previous classes) and with tripod masts. The 'M' group were destroyers *par excellence* for not only were they most handsome looking but they were also the first ever to mount turrets for their main armament.

With the opening of hostilities with the Axis powers in 1939 the shortage of destroyers was acute until UK yards could deliver the large number of vessels under construction. Therefore the 'Destroyers for Bases' agreement was ratified with the United States and fifty 'Flush Deckers' of 1918 vintage were delivered from American bases, although seven were immediately transferred to the Royal Canadian Navy.

HMS *Glamorgan* on builder's trials, testing her rate of advance. (MoD (Navy))

HMS *Norfolk* on builder's trials and showing that she is fitted with two bow anchors, unlike the later Type 42s which have to manage with one. (MoD (Navy))

In 1940 the destroyers were called upon to carry out a task for which they had certainly not been designed, yet 91,620 men of the British Expeditionary Force were evacuated home in the teeth of enemy opposition at Dunkirk.

From 1939, a short radius utility class had been under construction; known as the 'Hunt' class/es, they served well until and after the delivery of the first of the 'Obdurate' and 'Paladin' fleet destroyer classes. The 'O' class was well powered and fast, but as it had seemingly overtaken the Ordnance factories, the class had to mount the old type 4in gun.

The next two classes, 'Queensborough' and 'Rotherham', were of like design to the 'O' and 'P' classes, and all comprised eight ships each.

Following were the six utility construction classes commencing with HMS *Savage* (which bore in A position the prototype turret for the 'Battle' class) and ending with HMS *Zambesi*. The destroyers of these classes were all (with certain exceptions) armed with 4.7in guns in single shields. An innovation on the majority of these ships was the lattice or trellis foremast, and, about 1941, the first 'Hedgehog' anti-submarine weapon was mounted in HMS *Westcott*. With the 'Wager' or 'W' class of 1942, the 4.7in gun was mounted for the first time as the main armament of a destroyer, the 4.5in calibre of lower velocity being the replacement weapon, still at sea today.

Then came a large class of thirty-two destroyers which were allotted into four groups for naming purposes, these being the 'Ca', 'Co', 'Ch' and 'Cr' groups, the ships of which were not as the previous six classes and the last three groups had power-worked main armament.

Meanwhile a new and powerful destroyer design was under construction named the 'Battle' class. They were ships with all main armament forward of the bridge, in two power-worked turrets, being designed for tropical service and mounting a single 4in in a shield aft of the funnel. From the bridge aft was mounted a selection of heavy to light automatic AA weapons, not to forget the torpedo tubes – eight 21in as in most destroyers. They were large ships of 2,315 tons and length overall of 379ft. A later 'Battle' class was built, chiefly to the same designs but with improvements.

With the end of the war, destroyer building once again slowed and the 'Weapon' class of four ships was completed in 1948, this being a class which was like nothing that had gone before, reverting to two funnels and lower tonnage. Then followed a combination of 'Battle' and 'Weapon' designs to produce the 'Daring' class with square turrets for twin 4.5in guns and all welded construction, to produce the heaviest destroyer then known at 2,610 tons.

Finally there were the 'County' class guided missile destroyers which are definitely of light cruiser tonnage and similar to the Type 81s and have unique propulsion methods; the one and only Type 82 HMS *Bristol* with her three funnels; and the modern 'Town' class Type 42s with their improved follow-up class, the 'Stretched 42s', which are larger in all respects than the Type 45.

During the Falklands War of 1982 the Royal Navy experienced modern sea warfare, with attacks by jet aircraft on naval vessels, by means of long-range surface-to-surface missiles (namely the Exocet) and being bombed as in the Second World War at sea, so leading to the loss of HM Ships *Coventry* and *Sheffield*. The ships' radar could be improved, so in 2007 the first of a new Destroyer Class put to sea, being of the Type 45 DARING designation, with, it is hoped, infinitely better prospects of locating ones enemy and its missiles first. The propulsion of same is new; being gas turbine/electric, similar, in principle, to the diesel/electric CAPTAIN Classes of Destroyer Escorts from the USA of the Second World War. The new DARING Class is the first fighting ship of our Navy to be without steam turbines since they were introduced on the VIPER and VELOX (also Destroyers) of the C Class, *c*.1897–1902, yet the mode of Parsons Turbines is still relevant throughout the (E) Branch at Manadon*.

Details of all classes as completed, or as accepted, will be found on the appropriate page.

The destroyer HMS *Grenville*, having undergone conversion to frigate after the Second World War. (Fleet Photographic Unit, Portsmouth)

* Royal Naval Engineering College.

HMS *Daring* at speed in open water. (BAE Systems)

Royal Naval Destroyers 1893 to the Present Day

MIRANDA

After the Admiralty had persuaded the UK Government to purchase the manufacturing rights for Robert Whitehead's torpedo, a vessel capable of carrying and using the weapon had to be found. Therefore Messrs J.I. Thornycroft were asked to fit the weapon afloat, which they did by building a river launch of light construction capable of 16kts with a side/stern launching device to aim the torpedo. *Miranda* was not commissioned but acted as a trials vessel for the torpedo and the knowledge gained led to HMS *Lightning* Torpedo Boat No.1.

'A' CLASS

UNIT	COMPLETED	BUILDER	UNIT	COMPLETED	BUILDER
Ariel	1896	Thornycroft	*Janus*	1895	Palmers
Banshee	1894	Cammell Laird	*Lightning*	1895	Palmers
Boxer	1894	Thornycroft	*Lynx*	1894	Cammell Laird
Bruiser	1894	Thornycroft	*Opossum*	1895	Hawthorn
Charger	1894	Yarrow	*Porcupine*	1895	Palmers
Conflict	1894	White	*Ranger*	1895	Hawthorn
Contest	1894	Cammell Laird	*Rocket*	1894	Clydebank
Daring	1893	Thornycroft	*Salmon*	1895	Earle
Dasher	1895	Yarrow	*Shark*	1894	Clydebank
Decoy	1894	Thornycroft	*Skate*	1895	Vickers Armstrong (Barrow)
Dragon	1894	Cammell Laird	*Snapper*	1895	Earle
Ferret	1893	Cammell Laird	*Spitfire*	1895	Vickers Armstrong (Tyne)
Fervent	1895	Hanna Donald & Wilson	*Starfish*	1894	Vickers Armstrong (Barrow)
Handy	1894	Fairfield	*Sturgeon*	1894	Vickers Armstrong (Barrow)
Hardy	1894	Doxford	*Sunfish*	1895	Hawthorn
Hart	1894	Fairfield	*Surly*	1894	Clydebank
Hasty	1894	Yarrow	*Swordfish*	1895	Vickers Armstrong (Tyne)
Haughty	1895	Doxford	*Teazer*	1895	White
Havock	1893	Yarrow	*Wizard*	1895	White
Hornet	1893	Yarrow	*Zebra*	1895	Thames Iron Works
Hunter	1895	Fairfield	*Zephyr*	1895	Hanna Donald & Wilson

HMS *Dasher*, 'A' class torpedo boat destroyer, at sea in 1901. (R. Perkins)

Painting of HMS *Havock*, 'A' class, at sea. (Yarrow)

Displacement:	250-320 tons
Length:	200ft
Breadth:	19ft
Draught:	7ft
Armament:	*Main* One 12pdr
	Secondary Five 6pdr
	Tubes Two/three 14in
Machinery:	Triple expansion on two shafts giving 4,000ihp
Max speed:	27kts
Fuel:	60 tons coal

CLASS NOTES

Ships of this class were not all alike in appearance, the number of funnels varied from ship to ship. The bows towards the waterline tended to swell out into the familiar 'ram' shape of the period. Another recognition point was the turtle-back topped forecastle which was intended to clear the bow but actually dug them in in anything of a sea.

Some of the class, including HMS *Havock*, had locomotive boilers built into them. The correct marine boilers replaced these at a later date.

HMS *Daring*, *Decoy*, *Ferret*, *Havock*, *Hornet* and *Lynx* were built with a bow torpedo tube which tended to make them very wet.

HISTORICAL NOTES

HMS *Boxer* collided with HMS *Decoy* on 6 February 1918.

HMS *Havock* was later converted into the first submarine depot ship.

HMS *Lightning* was mined on 30 June 1915 in the North Sea.

'B' CLASS

UNIT	COMPLETED	BUILDER	UNIT	COMPLETED	BUILDER
Albacore	1908	Palmers	*Peterel*	1899	Palmers
Arab	1901	Clydebank	*Quail*	1895	Cammell Laird
Bonetta	1908	Palmers	*Seal*	1897	Cammell Laird
Earnest	1896	Cammell Laird	*Sparrowhawk*	1896	Cammell Laird
Express	1896	Cammell Laird	*Spiteful*	1898	Palmers
Griffon	1896	Cammell Laird	*Sprightly*	1901	Cammell Laird
Kangaroo	1901	Palmers	*Success*	1901	Doxford
Lively	1901	Cammell Laird	*Syren*	1901	Palmers
Locust	1896	Cammell Laird	*Thrasher*	1896	Cammell Laird
Myrmidon	1896	Cammell Laird	*Virago*	1896	Cammell Laird
Orwell	1901	Cammell Laird	*Wolf*	1897	Cammell Laird
Panther	1897	Cammell Laird			

Displacement:	355-470 tons
Length:	210ft
Breadth:	21ft
Draught:	5ft 6in
Armament:	*Main* One 12pdr
	Secondary Five 6pdr
	Tubes Two 18in
Machinery:	Triple expansion on three shafts giving 6,000ihp
Max speed:	30 kts
Fuel:	80 tons coal

CLASS NOTES

The 'B' class torpedo boat destroyers, being of one third greater tonnage than the 'A' class although of similar armament, had the advantage of three knots from 'down below' in excess of the previous class. They also had more of a unified appearance, each having four funnels, although their spacing was different. Although rated for 30kts, speed had to be reduced in even slightly mediocre weather and the class had little reserve hull strength. *Albacore, Arab, Bonetta* and *Express* were turbine-powered giving 6,000–9,000shp making 26.75–31kts.

HISTORICAL NOTES

HMS *Myrmidon* was lost by collision with the SS *Hambourne* in the English Channel on 26 March 1917.

HMS *Success* was wrecked off Fifeness on 27 December 1914 and was the first destroyer lost in the First World War.

HMS *Locust*, 'B' class, leaving harbour in 1908. (R. Perkins)

HMS *Thrasher*, 'B' class, at anchor in 1897. (R. Perkins)

'C' CLASS

UNIT	COMPLETED	BUILDER
Albatross	1898	Thornycroft
Avon	1896	Vickers Armstrong (Barrow)
Bat	1896	Palmers
Bittern	1897	Vickers Armstrong (Barrow)
Brazen	1896	Clydebank
Bullfinch	1901	Earle
Chamois	1896	Palmers
Cheerful	1897	Hawthorn
Cobra	1900	Vickers Armstrong (Tyne)
Crane	1896	Palmers
Dove	1898	Earle
Electra	1901	Clydebank
Fairy	1897	Fairfield
Falcon	1901	Fairfield
Fawn	1897	Palmers
Flirt	1897	Palmers
Flying Fish	1897	Palmers

UNIT	COMPLETED	BUILDER
Gipsy	1897	Fairfield
Greyhound	1900	Hawthorn
Kestrel	1898	Clydebank
Lee	1899	Doxford
Leopard	1897	Vickers Armstrong (Barrow)
Leven	1901	Fairfield
Mermaid	1898	Hawthorn
Osprey	1897	Fairfield
Ostrich	1901	Fairfield
Otter	1896	Vickers Armstrong (Barrow)
Racehorse	1900	Hawthorn
Recruit	1901	Clydebank
Roebuck	1901	Hawthorn
Star	1896	Palmers
Sylvia	1897	Doxford
Thorn	1901	Yarrow
Tiger	1901	Clydebank

UNIT	COMPLETED	BUILDER
Velox	1902	Hawthorn
Vigilant	1901	Clydebank
Violet	1897	Doxford
Viper	1899	Hawthorn

UNIT	COMPLETED	BUILDER
Vixen	1901	Vickers Armstrong (Barrow)
Vulture	1898	Clydebank
Whiting	1896	Palmers

Displacement:	345-400 tons
Length:	210ft
Breadth:	21ft
Draught:	9ft
Armament:	*Main* One 12pdr
	Secondary Five 6pdr
	Tubes Two 18in
Machinery:	Triple expansion on two shafts giving 6,000ihp
Max speed:	30kts
Fuel:	80 tons coal

CLASS NOTES

As with the 'B' class these ships were quite heavily armed, the 12-pounder being in A position forward of the bridge. The 6-pounders were positioned two each side aft of the first and third funnels and one on the stern. All ships had a light pole foremast with a short derrick immediately behind the conning position. The funnels were equidistant with the first and third of less diameter than the second but all being of the same height. The tubes were aft, one either beam.

HMS *Viper* and *Velox* were powered by turbines on four shafts with two screws, one inboard and one outboard of the A bracket on each shaft.

HMS *Cobra* featured an outboard rudder secured to the transom stern with the above-water section tapering to take a fitting for emergency steering.

HISTORICAL NOTES

HMS *Bittern* was lost through damage sustained after collision with the SS *Kenilworth* off Portland Bill on 4 April 1918.

HMS *Chamois* was the victim of a rather unusual mechanical failure, in that the tip of a propeller blade broke off whilst the ship was underway and, due to its impetus, the fragment penetrated the underwater hull aft of the A bracket which caused flooding of the stern and successive compartments until she foundered.

HMS *Cheerful* was mined on 30 June 1917 off the Shetlands.

HMS *Fairy* sank through damage sustained after ramming UC75 on 31 May 1918 in the North Sea.

HMS *Falcon* sank after collision with the *St John Fitzgerald* on 1 April 1918 in the North Sea.

HMS *Flirt* was lost in action with German destroyers on 27 October 1918, being torpedoed.

HMS *Recruit* was torpedoed by a UB16 on 1 May 1915 off the Galloper in the Thames.

HMS *Velox* was mined on 25 October 1915 off the Nab Light Vessel.

HMS *Velox*, 'C' class, making way in 1904. (R. Perkins)

'TAKU' CLASS

Unit:	*Taku* (ex-*Hai Nju*)
Completed:	1898
Builder:	Schichau (Elbing)
Displacement:	305 tons
Length:	194ft
Breadth:	20ft

Draught:	6ft
Armament:	*Main* Six 3pdr
	Tubes Three 18in
Machinery:	Triple expansion on two shafts giving 6,500ihp
Max speed:	30kts

CLASS NOTES

The only vessel of this class to serve with the Royal Navy, HMS *Taku* was of low freeboard with two large, raked funnels and light pole fore and main masts. The bow was 'ram'-shaped and the hull had curved topsides for the greater part of the main deck.

HISTORICAL NOTES

This vessel was taken over as a prize in 1900 from the Chinese Navy at about the time of the Boxer Rising. Renamed *Taku* to commemorate the attack on the forts of the same name in the same year, she was sold out of the Service at Hong Kong on 25 October 1916.

'D' CLASS

UNIT	COMPLETED
Angler	1896
Ariel	1897
Coquette	1897
Cygnet	1898
Cynthia	1898

UNIT	COMPLETED
Desperate	1895
Fame	1896
Foam	1896
Mallard	1896
Stag	1899

Builders:	Thornycroft
Displacement:	355-370 tons
Length:	210ft
Breadth:	21ft
Draught:	7ft 2.4in
Armament:	*Main* One 12pdr

Secondary Five 6pdr
Tubes Two 18in aft

Machinery:	Triple expansion on two shafts giving 5,800ihp
Max speed:	30kts
Fuel:	80 tons coal

CLASS NOTES

The ships of this class were the only ones of the 1896 building with two funnels, but in common with the 'B' and 'C' classes had as a recognition feature turtle-back topped bows and large ventilators between the funnels. Ships of this class saved considerable weight by being constructed from a new specification of steel which added strength to the hull.

HISTORICAL NOTES

HMS *Coquette* was mined and sank on 7 March 1915 in the North Sea.

HMS *Cygnet*, 'D' class, entering harbour in 1909. (R. Perkins)

'E' CLASS

UNIT	COMPLETED	BUILDER
Arun	1903	Cammell Laird
Blackwater	1903	Cammell Laird
Boyne	1904	Hawthorn
Chelmer	1904	Thornycroft
Cherwell	1903	Palmers
Colne	1905	Thornycroft
Dee	1905	Palmers

UNIT	COMPLETED	BUILDER
Derwent	1904	Hawthorn
Doon	1904	Hawthorn
Eden	1903	Hawthorn
Erne	1903	Palmers
Ettrick	1903	Palmers
Exe	1903	Palmers
Foyle	1903	Cammell Laird

UNIT	COMPLETED	BUILDER
Gala	1905	Yarrow
Garry	1905	Yarrow
Itchen	1903	Cammell Laird
Jed	1904	Thornycroft
Kale	1904	Hawthorn
Kennet	1903	Thornycroft
Liffey	1904	Cammell Laird
Moy	1904	Cammell Laird
Ness	1905	White
Nith	1905	White
Ouse	1905	Cammell Laird
Ribble	1904	Yarrow
Rother	1904	Palmers
Stour	1909	Cammell Laird
Swale	1905	Palmers
Test	1909	Cammell Laird
Teviot	1903	Yarrow
Ure	1904	Palmers
Usk	1903	Yarrow
Waveney	1903	Hawthorn
Wear	1905	Palmers
Welland	1904	Yarrow

Displacement:	550 tons
Length:	225ft
Breadth:	23ft 6in
Draught:	10ft
Armament:	*Main* Four 12pdr
	Tubes Two 18in
Machinery:	Triple expansion on two shafts giving 7,000ihp
Max speed:	25.5kts
Fuel:	120 tons coal

CLASS NOTES

In this design can be seen the typical 'destroyer' hull outline with a raised forecastle. The ships of this class had either two or four funnels, the four funnels being in pairs. One of the tubes was sited aft and one on the centreline between the funnels.

HMS *Eden* had turbines with three screws on each of her two shafts.

HMS *Stour* and *Test* were powered by turbines.

Two ships of similar design named *Bonetta* and *Albacore* were constructed 1908–10 to replace *Gala* and *Tiger*. These ships were of the following particulars: length 216ft, beam 21ft, mean draught 7ft 6in. They were powered by turbines of 6,000shp giving 27kts. They displaced 440 tons and had three 12-pounders and two 21in tubes. At 14kts they had approximately 2,000 miles radius. They were both coal fired.

HISTORICAL NOTES

HMS *Derwent* was mined off Le Havre on 2 May 1917.

HMS *Eden* sank after collision with the SS *France* in the English Channel on 17 June 1916.

HMS *Erne* was wrecked off Rattray Head near Aberdeen on 6 February 1915.

HMS *Foyle* was mined in the Straits of Dover on 15 March 1917.

HMS *Gala* and HMS *Tiger* sank after collisions in 1908 (see Appendix 4).

HMS *Itchen* was torpedoed by U99 on 6 July 1917 in the North Sea.

HMS *Kale* was mined in the North Sea on 27 March 1918.

HMS *Derwent*, 'E' class, at sea in 1898. (R. Perkins)

HMS *Welland*, 'E' class, at anchor in 1909. Note detail of transmitting/receiving aerials. (R. Perkins)

'F' CLASS

UNIT	COMPLETED	BUILDER
Afridi	1907	Vickers Armstrong (Tyne)
Amazon	1908	Thornycroft
Cossack	1907	Cammell Laird
Crusader	1909	White
Ghurka	1907	Hawthorn
Maori	1909	Denny
Mohawk	1907	White
Nubian	1909	Thornycroft
Saracen	1908	White
Tartar	1907	Thornycroft
Viking	1909	Palmers
Zulu	1909	Hawthorn

Displacement:	870-970 tons
Length:	250-290ft
Breadth:	26ft
Draught:	9ft
Armament:	*Main* Two 4in or five 12pdr
	Tubes Two 18in
Machinery:	Turbines on two/three shafts giving 14,000-15,500shp
Max speed:	35kts
Fuel:	80-100 tons oil

CLASS NOTES

All twelve of these vessels were different. Their funnels varied in number from three to six. (HMS *Viking* was the ship with six in three pairs of two.) This class saw the introduction of heavier armament on certain ships together with an increase of speed of over 5 kts on all earlier torpedo boat destroyers.

HISTORICAL NOTES

The Dover Patrol was well served by this class and the well-known case of 'ship surgery' was performed on the battle-scarred fore part of *Zulu* and the after part of *Nubian*. The renaming question was solved by giving the joined portions which now made up a new destroyer the name of *Zubian*.

HMS *Ghurka* was mined on 8 February 1917 four miles south-east of Dungeness Buoy.

HMS *Maori* was mined two miles north-west of Wirlingen Light Ship near Zeebrugge on 7 May 1915.

HMS *Nubian* was torpedoed by German destroyers on 27 October 1916 whilst in action off Folkestone, but was towed into port.

HMS *Zulu* struck a mine on 27 October 1916 but was towed back into port.

HMS *Cossack*, 'F' class, at anchor in 1911. (R. Perkins)

'SWIFT' CLASS

Unit:	*Swift*
Completed:	1907
Builder:	Cammell Laird
Displacement:	1,825 tons
	2,207 tons (full load)
Length:	353ft
Breadth:	34ft 6in
Draught:	10ft 6in
Armament:	*Main* Four 4in guns
	Secondary One 2pdr
	Tubes Two 18in
Machinery:	Turbines on four shafts giving 30,000shp
Max speed:	36kts
Fuel:	180 tons oil

CLASS NOTES

HMS *Swift* was a prototype for a class of ocean-going destroyers but she remained the only one of this design. She had three large circular raked funnels and during builder's trials she attained the speed of 39kts.

HISTORICAL NOTES

HMS *Swift* served as a leader during her time in the Dover Patrol 1914–18. After modernisation she mounted one 6in gun on the forecastle in place of the two forward 4in and her 18in tubes were changed to 21in. The 4in guns were the equivalent of 25-pounders. HMS *Swift* is the only destroyer in the Royal Navy ever to have mounted a 6in calibre gun and she was not approached in size until 1937.

HMS *Swift* in Dover Harbour. Note modifications made in 1916, 6in gun in lieu of two 4in guns, new foremast and topmast, 10in signalling searchlights on wings of bridge, 20in searchlight abaft No.3 funnel, AA Pom-Pom, enormous cowls. (IWM)

'G' CLASS

UNIT	COMPLETED	BUILDER
Basilisk	1910	White
Beagle	1909	Clydebank
Bulldog	1909	Clydebank
Foxhound	1909	Clydebank
Grampus (ex-*Nautilus*)	1910	Thames Ironworks
Grasshopper	1909	Fairfield
Harpy	1909	White
Mosquito	1910	Fairfield
Pincher	1910	Denny
Racoon	1910	Cammell Laird
Rattlesnake	1910	Harland & Wolff (Clyde)
Renard	1909	Cammell Laird
Savage	1910	Thornycroft
Scorpion	1910	Fairfield
Scourge	1910	Hawthorn
Wolverine	1910	Cammell Laird

Displacement:	860-940 tons
Length:	275ft
Breadth:	28ft
Draught:	8.5ft
Armament:	*Main* One 4in
	Secondary Three 12pdr
	Tubes Two 21in
Machinery:	Turbine on two/three shafts giving 12,500shp
Max speed:	27kts
Fuel:	120 tons coal

HMS *Bulldog*, 'G' class, 1910. Note A gun on raised deckhouse. (R. Perkins)

HMS *Savage*, 'G' class at sea in 1911. (R. Perkins)

These ships were coal burning, there apparently being concern over oil stocks in the event of war. A further point of interest is that with the exception of HMS *Swift* (qv) this was the first class to carry the 21in torpedo; additionally, this was the last destroyer class built for the Royal Navy to be coal fuelled.

CLASS NOTES
The ships of this class were all more or less uniform in appearance. The 4in was mounted on its own shelter deck where it was able to be fought in short, steep seas, being on a drier deck. The bridge was improved being more square and higher. One tube was just forward of the main mast, and the other positioned on the stern.

HISTORICAL NOTES
HMS *Pincher* was wrecked on the Seven Stones on 24 July 1918.

HMS *Racoon* was wrecked on 4 January 1918 on the Irish Coast in a snowstorm.

HMS *Wolverine* was sunk after collision with HMS *Rosemary* (sloop) on 12 December 1917 off Lough Foyle.

'H' CLASS

UNIT	COMPLETED	BUILDER
Acorn	1910	Clydebank
Alarm	1910	Clydebank
Brisk	1910	Clydebank
Chameleon	1910	Clydebank
Comet	1910	Fairfield
Fury	1911	Inglis
Goldfinch	1910	Fairfield
Hope	1910	Swan Hunter
Larne	1910	Thornycroft
Lyra	1910	Thornycroft
Martin	1910	Thornycroft
Minstrel	1911	Thornycroft
Nemesis	1910	Hawthorn
Nereide	1910	Hawthorn
Nymphe	1911	Hawthorn
Redpole	1910	White
Rifleman	1910	White
Ruby	1910	White
Sheldrake	1911	Denny
Staunch	1910	Denny

HMS *Chameleon*, 'H' class, at sea in 1911. (R. Perkins)

HMS *Rifleman*, 'H' class, entering harbour in 1911. (R. Perkins)

Displacement:	730-780 tons
Length:	246ft 6in
Breadth:	25ft 6in
Draught:	7-10ft
Armament:	*Main* Two 4in
	Secondary Two 12pdr
	AA One 3pdr (in some)
	Tubes Two 21in
Machinery:	Turbines on three shafts giving 13,500shp
Max speed:	27kts
Fuel:	170 tons fuel oil

CLASS NOTES

These ships had one tall funnel abaft the foremast, and two shorter and broader ones further aft spaced apart. The first tube was on the centreline between the second and third funnels. One 4in was in position A and one in Y with the 12-pounders on either beam at the break of the forecastle.

HISTORICAL NOTES

HMS *Comet* was torpedoed 6 August 1918 by an Austrian U-boat in the Mediterranean.

HMS *Goldfinch* was wrecked on the night of 18/19 February 1915 in fog, at Start Point, Sanday Island, Orkneys.

HMS *Minstrel* and *Nemesis* were loaned to the Imperial Japanese Navy from 1917–18 and named HIM *Sendan* and *Kandan*.

HMS *Staunch* was torpedoed on 11 November 1917, by UC38 off Gaza, Palestine.

'I' CLASS

UNIT	COMPLETED	BUILDER	UNIT	COMPLETED	BUILDER
Acheron	1911	Thornycroft	*Beaver*	1911	Hawthorn
Archer	1911	Yarrow	*Defender*	1911	Denny
Ariel	1911	Thornycroft	*Druid*	1911	Denny
Attack	1911	Yarrow	*Ferret*	1911	White
Badger	1911	Hawthorn	*Firedrake*	1912	Yarrow

UNIT	COMPLETED	BUILDER
Forester	1911	White
Goshawk	1911	Beardmore
Hind	1911	Clydebank
Hornet	1911	Clydebank
Hydra	1912	Clydebank
Jackal	1911	Hawthorn
Lapwing	1911	Cammell Laird
Lizard	1911	Cammell Laird
Lurcher	1912	Yarrow
Oak	1912	Yarrow
Phoenix	1911	Vickers Armstrong (Barrow)
Sandfly	1911	Swan Hunter
Tigress	1911	Hawthorn

HMS *Lapwing*, 'I' class, 1913. Note main mast is vertical under strain from aerials, and the bands on the funnel denoting flotilla leader. (R. Perkins)

Displacement:	750-790 tons
Length:	246ft (*Acheron* 252ft)
Breadth:	26ft 9in (*Acheron* 26ft)
Draught:	8ft 6in (*Acheron* 9ft)
Armament:	*Main* Two 4in
	Secondary Two 12pdr
	AA One 3pdr
	Tubes Two 21in
Machinery:	Turbines on two shafts giving 16,500-20,000shp
Max speed:	30-32kts
Fuel:	150-180 tons oil

CLASS NOTES

Originally only twenty of this class were built but *Lurcher*, *Firedrake* and *Oak* brought the total to twenty-three after three ships were transferred to the Royal Australian Navy. All ships had two funnels of the same height with the exception of the latter three. Guns were mounted as in the 'H' class.

HMS *Archer* and *Attack* used steam at a higher temperature being superheated, and HMS *Badger* and *Beaver* were completed with geared turbines for trials.

HISTORICAL NOTES

HMS *Ariel* struck a mine whilst minelaying on 2 August 1918 in the North Sea.

HMS *Attack* was torpedoed by UC34 on 30 December 1917 off Alexandria.

HMS *Phoenix* was torpedoed by Austrian U-boat UXXVII on 14 May 1918 in the Adriatic.

'K' CLASS

UNIT	COMPLETED	BUILDER		UNIT	COMPLETED	BUILDER
Acasta	1912	Clydebank		*Sparrowhawk*	1912	Swan Hunter
Achates	1912	Clydebank		*Spitfire*	1913	Swan Hunter
Ambuscade	1913	Clydebank		*Unity*	1913	Thornycroft
Ardent	1913	Denny		*Victor*	1913	Thornycroft
Christopher	1912	Hawthorn				
Cockatrice	1912	Hawthorn				
Contest	1913	Hawthorn				
Fortune	1913	Fairfield				
Garland	1913	Cammell Laird				
Hardy	1912	Thornycroft				
Lynx	1912	Harland & Wolff				
Midge	1912	Harland & Wolff				
Owl	1912	Harland & Wolff				
Paragon	1913	Thornycroft				
Porpoise	1913	Thornycroft				
Shark	1912	Swan Hunter				

Displacement:	934-984 tons
Length:	267ft 6in
Breadth:	27ft
Draught:	9ft 6in (*Hardy* 8ft)
Armament:	*Main* Three 4in
	AA One 2pdr
	Tubes Two 21in (single mountings)
Machinery:	Turbines on two/three shafts giving 22,500-25,000shp
Max speed:	31kts
Fuel:	160-200 tons oil

CLASS NOTES

These ships had three funnels, all being circular, the first the tallest. The 4in guns were mounted in A position, on either beam of the second tube, or one before and one after the second tube. This was the last class to have mixed names. All following began with the same letter, subject to suitability.

HMS *Hardy* was fitted with a diesel engine for cruising.

HMS *Fortune*, although of this class in super-structure, was actually the prototype hull of the 'L' class, with a clipper bow.

HISTORICAL NOTES

HMS *Ardent* was sunk by gunfire from ships of the German High Seas Fleet in the Battle of Jutland on 1 June 1916.

HMS *Contest* was hit and sunk by gunfire by ships of the German High Seas Fleet in the Battle of Jutland, sinking about midnight 31 May/1 June 1916.

HMS *Lynx* was mined on 9 August 1915 in the Moray Firth.

HMS *Paragon* was torpedoed in action in the Straits of Dover, 18 March 1917, by a German destroyer.

HMS *Shark* was torpedoed after being hit by German light cruisers' gunfire in the Battle of Jutland 31 May 1916.

HMS *Sparrowhawk* was disabled during the Battle of Jutland after collision with HMS *Broke* and to avoid falling into enemy hands was torpedoed by HMS *Marksman* on 1 June 1916.

HMS *Porpoise*, 'K' class, at sea in 1914. (R. Perkins)

'L' CLASS

UNIT	COMPLETED	BUILDER	UNIT	COMPLETED	BUILDER
Laertes	1913	Swan Hunter	*Leonidas*	1913	Hawthorn
Laforey	1913	Fairfield	*Liberty*	1913	White
Lance	1914	Thornycroft	*Linnet*	1913	Yarrow
Landrail	1914	Yarrow	*Llewellyn*	1913	Beardmore
Lark	1913	Yarrow	*Lochinvar*	1915	Beardmore
Lassoo	1915	Beardmore	*Lookout*	1914	Thornycroft
Laurel	1913	White	*Louis*	1913	Fairfield
Laverock	1914	Yarrow	*Loyal*	1913	Denny
Lawford	1913	Fairfield	*Lucifer*	1913	Hawthorn
Legion	1914	Denny	*Lydiard*	1914	Hawthorn
Lennox	1914	Beardmore	*Lysander*	1913	Swan Hunter

HMS *Legion*, 'L' class, at sea in 1914. (R. Perkins)

HMS *Linnet*, 'L' class, standing by for sunset, 1914. (R. Perkins)

Displacement:	965-1,003 tons
Length:	269ft
Breadth:	26ft 9in
Draught:	9ft 6in
Armament:	*Main* Three 4in
	AA One 2pdr
	Tubes Four 21in (2 x 2)
Machinery:	Turbine on two shafts giving 24,500shp
	(22,500shp *Leonidas* and *Lucifer*)
Max speed:	29kts
Fuel:	200-290 tons oil

CLASS NOTES

Of this class sixteen ships had three funnels with the centre one broader than the other two, the remaining six ships having two funnels only. A searchlight was positioned between the tube mountings which were aft of the funnels. In the three-funnelled ships the second 4in gun was positioned between the second and third funnels upon a 'bandstand'.

All these vessels were allocated 'L' names, but each had been given a different name beforehand. In order listed these were: *Sarpedon*; *Florizel*; *Daring*; *Hotspur*; *Haughty*; *Magic*; *Redgauntlet*; *Hereward*; *Ivanhoe*; *Viola*; *Portia*; *Rob Roy*; *Rosalind*; *Havock*; *Picton*; *Malice*; *Dragon*; *Talisman*; *Orlando*; *Rocket*; *Waverley*; *Ulysses*.

HISTORICAL NOTES

HMS *Laforey* and *Leonidas* were the first torpedo boat destroyers to have geared turbines.

HMS *Laforey* was mined and sank in the English Channel on 23 March 1917.

HMS *Lance* is reputed to have fired the first shot of the First World War.

HMS *Lassoo* was torpedoed off the Maas Light Ship on 13 August 1916 by a German U-boat.

HMS *Legion* was equipped for minelaying.

HMS *Louis* was wrecked on 31 October 1915 in Suvla Bay.

ADMIRALTY 'M' CLASS

UNIT	COMPLETED	BUILDER	UNIT	COMPLETED	BUILDER
Maenad	1915	Denny	*Medina*		
Magic			(ex-*Redmill*)	1916	White
(ex-*Marigold*)	1916	White	*Medway*		
Mameluke	1915	Clydebank	(ex-*Redwing*)	1916	White
Mandate	1915	Fairfield	*Menace*	1916	Swan Hunter
Manners	1915	Fairfield	*Michael*	1915	Thornycroft
Marmion	1915	Swan Hunter	*Millbrook*	1915	Thornycroft
Marne	1915	Clydebank	*Milne*	1914	Clydebank
Martial	1915	Swan Hunter	*Mindful*	1915	Fairfield
Marvel	1915	Denny	*Minion*	1915	Thornycroft
Mary Rose	1916	Palmers	*Mischief*	1915	Fairfield
Matchless	1914	Swan Hunter	*Mons*	1915	Clydebank

UNIT	COMPLETED	BUILDER
Moorsom	1915	Clydebank
Moresby (ex-Marlion)	1916	White
Morris	1914	Clydebank
Munster (ex-Monitor)	1916	Thornycroft
Murray	1914	Palmers
Myngs	1915	Palmers
Mystic (ex-Myrtle)	1915	Denny
Napier	1916	Clydebank
Narborough	1916	Clydebank
Narwhal	1916	Denny
Negro	1916	Palmers
Nepean	1916	Thornycroft
Nereus	1916	Thornycroft
Nessus	1915	Swan Hunter
Nestor	1916	Swan Hunter
Nicator	1916	Denny
Nizam	1916	Stephen
Noble (ex-Nisus)	1916	Stephen
Nomad	1916	Stephen
Nonpareil	1916	Stephen (Completed by Beardmore)
Nonsuch (ex-Narcissus)	1916	Palmers
Norman	1916	Palmers
Norseman	1916	Doxford
Northesk	1916	Palmers
North Star	1917	Palmers
Nugent	1917	Palmers
Obdurate	1916	Scotts
Obedient	1916	Scotts
Oberon	1916	Doxford
Observer	1916	Fairfield

UNIT	COMPLETED	BUILDER
Octavia (ex-Onyx)	1916	Doxford
Offa	1916	Fairfield
Onslaught	1916	Fairfield
Onslow	1916	Fairfield
Opal	1916	Doxford
Ophelia	1916	Doxford
Opportune	1916	Doxford
Oracle	1916	Doxford
Orcadia	1916	Fairfield
Orestes	1916	Doxford
Orford	1916	Doxford
Oriana	1916	Fairfield
Oriole	1916	Palmers
Orpheus	1916	Doxford
Osiris	1916	Palmers
Ossory	1916	Clydebank
Paladin	1916	Scotts
Parthian	1916	Scotts
Partridge	1916	Swan Hunter
Pasley	1916	Swan Hunter
Pelican	1916	Beardmore
Pellew	1916	Beardmore
Penn	1916	Clydebank
Peregrin	1916	Clydebank
Petard	1916	Denny
Peyton	1916	Denny
Pheasant	1916	Fairfield
Phoebe	1916	Fairfield
Pigeon	1916	Hawthorn
Plover	1916	Hawthorn
Plucky	1916	Scotts
Portia	1916	Scotts
Prince	1916	Stephen
Pylades	1916	Stephen

HMS *Medina*, Admiralty 'M' class, in war colours, 1919. Note larger shield for A gun and pennant number. (R. Perkins)

Displacement:	994-1,042 tons
Length:	269ft
Breadth:	27ft 6in
Draught:	10ft 6in
Armament:	*Main* Three 4in
	AA One 2pdr
	Tubes Four 21in (2x2)
Machinery:	Turbines on three shafts giving 25,000shp
Max speed:	34kts
Fuel:	300 tons oil

CLASS NOTES

These were all three-funnelled ships, the funnels being of the same height, circular but narrow. Positioning of armament as for the 'L' class. A number of the earlier destroyers of this class had cruising turbines which were omitted from later buildings.

HMS *Partridge, Norman, Maenad, Ophelia* and *Observer* were fitted out to carry a kite balloon.

HISTORICAL NOTES

HMS *Marmion* sank on 21 October 1917 after collision with HMS *Tirade* off the Shetlands.

HMS *Mary Rose* was sunk by gunfire from the German light cruisers SMS *Bremse* and *Brummer* on 17 October 1917 off the Norwegian coast in a convoy action.

HMS *Narborough* sank with HMS *Opal* in a storm on 12 January 1918 outside Scapa Flow.

HMS *Negro* sank on 21 December 1916 after collision with HMS *Hoste* in the North Sea during bad weather.

HMS *Nessus* sank after colliding with HMS *Amphitrite* on 8 September 1918 in bad weather in the North Sea.

HMS *Nestor* was sunk by gunfire from ships of the German High Seas Fleet on 31 May 1916 during the Battle of Jutland.

HMS *Nomad* was sunk by gunfire by the ships of the German High Seas Fleet on 31 May 1916.

HMS *North Star* was sunk at Zeebrugge by gunfire from German shore batteries on 23 April 1918.

HMS *Partridge* was sunk by gunfire on 12 December 1917 during an action with four German destroyers guarding a convoy off the Norwegian coast.

HMS *Pheasant* was mined and sank, 1 March 1917, off the Orkneys.

HMS *Offa*, Admiralty 'M' class, in war colours in 1916. (R. Perkins)

HAWTHORN 'M' CLASS

Units:	*Mansfield, Mentor*	Armament:	*Main* Three 4in	
Completed:	1915		*AA* One 2pdr	
Builder:	Hawthorn Leslie		*Tubes* Four 21in (2x2)	
Displacement:	1,057 tons	Machinery:	Turbines on three shafts giving	
Length:	271ft		27,000shp	
Breadth:	27ft 6in	Max speed:	35kts	
Draught:	10ft 6in	Fuel:	300 tons oil	

CLASS NOTES

A Hawthorn derivative of the Admiralty 'M' design. The second 4in was situated aft of the second funnel and forward of the third. The funnels were in pairs. The tubes were in pairs and mounted on the centreline.

HMS *Mansfield*, Hawthorn 'M' class, at sea in 1916. (IWM)

YARROW 'M' CLASS

UNIT	COMPLETED
Manley	1914
Minos	1914
Miranda	1914
Moon	1915
Morning Star	1915
Mounsey	1915
Musketeer	1915
Nerissa	1916
Relentless	1916
Rival	1916

Builder:	Yarrow
Displacement:	879-898 tons
Length:	271ft
Breadth:	27ft
Draught:	10ft 6in
Armament:	*Main* Three 4in
	AA One 2pdr
	Tubes Four 21in (2x2)
Machinery:	Turbine on two shafts giving 25,000-27,000shp
Max speed:	36kts
Fuel:	200-230 tons oil

CLASS NOTES

All ships had two funnels, the foremost broader than the aft one. Apart from this they were similar to the Admiralty 'M' class of 1914. These ships had a straight stern.

HMS *Moon, Mounsey* and *Musketeer* were fitted out to carry a kite balloon.

HMS *Minos*, Yarrow 'M' class, entering harbour in 1914. (R. Perkins)

HMS *Relentless*, Yarrow 'M' class, entering harbour in 1914. (R. Perkins)

THORNYCROFT 'M' CLASS

UNIT	COMPLETED
Mastiff	1914
Meteor	1914
Patrician	1916
Patriot	1916
Rapid	1916
Ready	1916

Builder:	Thornycroft
Displacement:	985-1,070 tons
Length:	274ft
Breadth:	27ft 6in
Draught:	10ft 6in
Armament:	*Main* Three 4in
	AA One 2pdr
	Tubes Four 21in (2x2)
Machinery:	Turbines on two shafts giving 25,000-27,000shp
Max speed:	35kts
Fuel:	300 tons oil

CLASS NOTES

These ships were similar to those of the 'L' class of 1913 but all had three funnels. All of this class were a derivation of the Admiralty 'M' design of 1914 which were enlargements of the 'L' class.

HMS *Patriot* was fitted out to carry a kite balloon.

HMS *Rapid*, Thornycroft 'M' class, leaving harbour in 1924. Note the enclosed after conning position. (R. Perkins)

HMS *Ready*, Thornycroft 'M' class, at anchor in 1918. (R. Perkins)

EX-TURKISH NEW BUILDINGS

Units:	Talisman (ex-Napier), Termagant (ex-Narborough), Trident (ex-Offa), Turbulent (ex-Ogre)	Breadth:	28ft 6in
		Draught:	9ft 6in
		Armament:	Main Five 4in
			Tubes Four 21in (2x2)
Completed:	1916	Machinery:	Turbines on three shafts giving 25,000shp
Builder:	Hawthorn Leslie	Max speeds:	32kts
Displacement:	1,098 tons	Fuel:	238 tons oil
Length:	309ft		

CLASS NOTES

All of these ships frequently acted as leaders. The positioning of the 4in guns was rather peculiar: in A position on the forecastle two 4in guns were mounted side-by-side, a further 4in was mounted between the first pair of funnels, the fourth was aft of the tubes and the fifth 4in surmounting a 'bandstand' on the quarterdeck. They were very successful ships, seaworthy and the design proved to be the basis for the Admiralty 'V' and 'W' classes. Depth charges were carried.

HISTORICAL NOTES

HMS *Turbulent* sank during the Battle of Jutland after colliding with a large unidentified German Vessel on 31 May 1916.

EX-GREEK NEW BUILDINGS

UNIT	BUILDER
Medea (ex-Kriti)	Clydebank
Medusa (ex-Lesvos)	Clydebank
Melampus (ex-Chios)	Fairfield
Melpomene (ex-Samos)	Fairfield

Completed:	1915
Displacement:	1,040 tons
Length:	273ft 6in
Breadth:	26ft 6in
Draught:	10ft 6in
Armament:	Main Three 4in
	Tubes Four 21in (2x2)
Machinery:	Turbines on three shafts giving 25,000shp
Max speed:	32 kts
Fuel:	270 tons oil

CLASS NOTES

In these ships the foremast was shorter than the main and the fore funnel taller than the second and third.

HISTORICAL NOTES

HMS *Medusa* was lost in a collision on the 25 March 1916 with HMS *Laverock* off the Schlieswig Coast.

HMS *Melampus* (ex-Greek) at sea in 1914. (R. Perkins)

EX-CHILEAN NEW BUILDINGS

Units:	Tipperary (ex-Almirante Riveres), Botha (ex-Almirante Williams Rebelledo), Broke (ex-Almirante Goni), Faulknor (ex-Almirante Simpson)
Completed:	1914 (Tipperary 1915)
Builders:	White
Displacement:	1,700-1,850 tons average
Length:	331ft 6in
Breadth:	32ft 6in
Draught:	11ft
Armament:	*Main* Two 4.7in
	Secondary Two 4in
	AA Two 2pdr
	Tubes Four 21in (2x2)
Machinery:	Turbines on three shafts giving 36,000shp
Max speed:	32kts
Fuel:	403 tons coal; 83 tons oil

CLASS NOTES

All these ships had four funnels, the first tall and narrow, the other three being equally spaced but shorter. The ships of this class were rated as leaders. HMS *Botha* had tubes in single mountings. All ships of this class originally had four 4in and 2-pounder AA guns.

HISTORICAL NOTES

HMS *Tipperary* was sunk by gunfire from ships of the German High Seas Fleet at the Battle of Jutland on 31 May 1916.

HMS *Broke* (ex-Chilean) in 1914. Note two single guns in A position abeam of the bridge and on the stern. (R. Perkins)

'MARKSMAN' CLASS

UNIT	COMPLETED	BUILDER
Abdiel	1916	Cammell Laird
Gabriel	1916	Cammell Laird
Ithuriel	1916	Cammell Laird
Kempenfelt	1915	Cammell Laird
Lightfoot	1915	White
Marksman	1915	Hawthorn Leslie
Nimrod	1915	Denny

Displacement:	1,600 tons average
Length:	321ft
Breadth:	31ft 9in
Draught:	11ft
Armament:	*Main* Four 4in
	AA Two 2pdr
	Tubes Four 21in (2x2)
Machinery:	Turbines on three shafts giving 36,000shp
Max speed:	34kts
Fuel:	510 tons oil

CLASS NOTES

All were four-funnelled ships, the first funnel being taller than the others. The guns were in A position and between the first, second and third funnels. HMS *Abdiel* was a minelayer with no stern gun or tubes and all funnels of equal height. She was armed with three 4in guns, and was screened from the fourth funnel to the stern on the main deck to give shelter for sixty to seventy mines.

HMS *Gabriel* was also later fitted out as a minelayer and carried seventy-two mines.

Below top: HMS *Abdiel*, 'Marksman' class, flying pennant number in 1926. (R. Perkins)

Below bottom: HMS *Nimrod*, 'Marksman' class, 1924. Note flying pennant number with unusual pattern of aerial. (R. Perkins)

'ANZAC' CLASS

Units:	Anzac, Grenville, Hoste, Parker (ex-Frobisher), Saumarez, Seymour
Completed:	1916 (Anzac 1917)
Builder:	Cammell Laird (Anzac Denny)
Displacement:	1,670 tons
Length:	325ft
Breadth:	31ft 9in
Draught:	10ft 6in
Armament:	*Main* four 4in (director controlled)
	Secondary Two 2pdr
	AA One 3in
	Tubes Four 21in (2x2)
Machinery:	Turbine on three shafts giving 36,000shp
Max speed:	34kts
Fuel:	415 tons oil

CLASS NOTES

These were all three-funnelled ships – the first funnel being taller and thicker than any of the others. Two of the 4in guns were positioned on the fore deck in A and B position, superimposed. These ships were built as leaders.

HISTORICAL NOTES

HMS *Anzac* was presented to the Government of Australia for use by the RAN in 1919.

HMS *Hoste* was lost after a collision on 21 December 1916 in the North Sea.

HMS *Saumarez*, 'Anzac' class, 1919. Note A and B guns superimposed. (R. Perkins)

HMS *Anzac*, 'Anzac' class, 1919. Note A and B guns superimposed. (R. Perkins)

'ARNO' CLASS

Unit:	Arno (ex-Liz)
Commenced:	1914
Completed:	1915
Builders:	Ansaldo (Genoa)
Displacement:	520 tons
Length:	32ft
Breadth:	23ft 6in
Draught:	7ft
Armament:	*Main* Four 3in (12pdr)
	Tubes Three 18in (1x3)
Machinery:	Turbines on two shafts giving 8,000shp
Max speed:	28.5kts
Fuel:	130 tons oil

British need for destroyer tonnage at that time. The two forward 3in guns were positioned on the fore deck in A position close to the base of the tall bridge. The third 3in gun was positioned at the rear of the funnel and the fourth 3in was positioned on the stern.

HMS *Arno* was a good-looking ship with straight stem and two funnels and inward sloping topsides towards the stern. Although smaller than the conventional British destroyer of the time, she was a well-built ship with a number of good features including high freeboard and tall protective bridge.

CLASS NOTES

This destroyer was purchased whilst still building from the Portuguese government, such was the

HISTORICAL NOTES

HMS *Arno* was lost by collision with HMS *Hope* (destroyer) in the Dardanelles on 23 March 1918.

HMS *Arno* (ex-Portuguese) leaving Grand Harbour Valletta in 1916. (IWM)

ADMIRALTY 'R' CLASS

UNIT	COMPLETED	BUILDER	UNIT	COMPLETED	BUILDER
Radstock	1916	Swan Hunter	Sarpedon	1916	Hawthorn
Raider	1916	Swan Hunter	Satyr	1917	Beardmore
Recruit	1917	Doxford	Sceptre	1917	Stephen
Redgauntlet	1917	Denny	Setter	1917	Beardmore
Redoubt	1917	Doxford	Sharpshooter	1917	Beardmore
Restless	1916	Clydebank	Simoon	1916	Clydebank
Rigorous	1916	Clydebank	Skate	1917	Clydebank
Rob Roy	1916	Denny	Skilful	1917	Harland & Wolff
Rocket	1916	Denny	Sorceress	1916	Swan Hunter
Romola	1916	Clydebank	Springbok	1917	Harland & Wolff
Rowena	1916	Clydebank	Starfish	1916	Hawthorn
Sable	1916	White	Stork	1917	Hawthorn
Salmon	1916	Harland & Wolff	Sturgeon	1917	Stephen

UNIT	COMPLETED	BUILDER		UNIT	COMPLETED	BUILDER
Sylph	1917	Harland & Wolff		*Thisbe*	1917	Hawthorn
Tancred	1917	Beardmore		*Thruster*	1917	Hawthorn
Tarpon	1917	Clydebank		*Tormentor*	1917	Stephen
Telemachus	1917	Clydebank		*Tornado*	1917	Stephen
Tempest	1917	Fairfield		*Torrent*	1917	Swan Hunter
Tenacious	1917	Harland & Wolff		*Torrid*	1917	Swan Hunter
Tetrarch	1917	Harland & Wolff				

Displacement:	1,040 tons
Length:	276ft
Breadth:	26ft 9in
Draught:	10ft 6in
Armament:	*Main* Three 4in
	AA One 2pdr, one MG
	Tubes Four 21in (2x2)
Machinery:	Geared turbines on two shafts giving 27,000shp
Max speed:	36kts
Fuel:	285-300 tons oil

CLASS NOTES

These ships were similar to the Admiralty 'M' class in appearance, the difference being the after 4in gun in a bandstand and the curved sloping stern.

HISTORICAL NOTES

HMS *Recruit* sank after being mined on 9 August 1917 in the North Sea.

HMS *Salmon* was renamed *Sable* in 1933, and HMS *Sable* was renamed HMS *Salmon* in the same year.

HMS *Setter* sank after colliding with HMS *Sylph* in fog off Harwich on 17 May 1917.

HMS *Simoon* was sunk by gunfire from German destroyers off Schouwen Bank on 23 January 1917.

HMS *Tarpon* and *Telemachus* were fitted out as minelayers.

HMS *Tornado* and *Torrent* were mined and sunk on the night of 22/23 December 1917 off the Maas Light Ship.

HMS *Skate*, Admiralty 'R' class, 1917. Note symmetrical fore and main masts.

HMS *Tarpon*, Admiralty 'R' class, 1924. Note larger gun shield on A gun and minelaying rails at the stern. (R. Perkins)

YARROW LATER 'M' CLASS

UNIT	COMPLETED
Sabrina	1916
Strongbow	1916
Surprise	1916
Sybille	1917
Truculent	1917
Tyrant	1917
Ulleswater	1917

Builder:	Yarrow
Displacement:	897-923 tons
Length:	271ft 6in
Breadth:	25ft 9in
Draught:	10ft 6in
Armament:	*Main* three 4in
	Secondary One 2pdr
	Tubes Four 21in (2x2)
Machinery:	Turbines on two shafts giving 27,000shp
Max speed:	36kts
Fuel:	215-260 tons oil

CLASS NOTES

All these ships had a likeness to their predecessors, the earlier Yarrow 'M' class; they were, however, of narrower beam, greater tonnage and had sloping sterns.

HISTORICAL NOTES

HMS *Strongbow* was sunk by gunfire from the German light cruisers SMS *Bremse* and *Brummer* off the Norwegian coast in a convoy action on 17 October 1917.

HMS *Surprise* was mined off the Maas Light Ship on the night of 22/23 December 1917.

HMS *Ulleswater* was torpedoed by a German U-boat (UC17) off the Dutch coast on 15 August 1918.

HMS *Truculent*, Yarrow later 'M' class, at sea in 1924. (R. Perkins)

HMS *Tyrant*, Yarrow later 'M' class, at sea in 1924. (R. Perkins)

THORNYCROFT 'R' CLASS

Units:	Radiant, Retriever, Rosalind, Taurus, Teazer
Completed:	1917 (Rosalind 1916)
Builder:	Thornycroft
Displacement:	1,034-1,064 tons
Length:	274ft
Breadth:	27ft
Draught:	11 ft
Armament:	Main Three 4in
	Secondary One 2pdr
	Tubes Four 21in (2x2)
	AS 30 300lb DCs carried
Machinery:	Turbines on two shafts giving 29,000shp
Max speed:	35kts
Fuel:	285-320 tons oil

CLASS NOTES

These ships were similar to the 'M' class built by Thornycroft in 1914, the main difference being that the after 4in was on a 'bandstand'. All ships of this class had three funnels, the second funnel being broader than the first and third, all raked and capped. On trials HMS *Teazer* is said to have exceeded 40kts and all others of this class surpassed their contract speed. The 4in guns of this and previous classes had an elevation of 20°.

HMS *Radiant* later became the *Phra Ruang* of the Royal Siamese Navy.

HMS *Radiant* at her mooring. (R. Perkins)

HMS *Rosalind* at her mooring. (R. Perkins)

ADMIRALTY MODIFIED 'R' CLASS

UNIT	BUILDER		
Tirade	Scotts	Ulysses	Doxford
Tower	Swan Hunter	Umpire	Doxford
Trenchant	White	Undine	Fairfield
Tristram	White	Urchin	Palmers
Ulster	Beardmore	Ursa	Palmers
		Ursula	Scotts

Completed:	1917
Displacement:	1,085 tons
Length:	276ft
Breadth:	26ft 9in
Draught:	11ft
Armament:	*Main* Three 4in
	Secondary One 2pdr
	Tubes Four 21in (2x2)
Machinery:	Geared turbines on two shafts giving 27,000shp
Max speed:	36kts
Fuel:	280 tons oil

CLASS NOTES

This class was a combination of the designs of two previous classes – the Yarrow 'M' and the Admiralty 'R'. The ships had two funnels, the aftermost being of lesser diameter and the bridge structure was also higher.

Above the second pair of tubes was a searchlight which trained with them. The after 4in gun was in X position on a 'bandstand'. HMS *Ulster* and *Ursa* had 30° elevation on the main 4in armament.

HISTORICAL NOTES

HMS *Ulysses* sank after a collision with SS *Ellerie* (merchant ship) in the Firth of Clyde on 29 October 1918. She was the last Royal Navy destroyer to be lost in the First World War.

HMS *Trenchant*, Admiralty modified 'R' class, 1924. Note ribs on forefunnel. (R. Perkins)

HMS *Umpire*, Admiralty modified 'R' class, underway in 1918. (R. Perkins)

ADMIRALTY 'S' CLASS

UNIT	COMPLETED	BUILDER	UNIT	COMPLETED	BUILDER
Sabre	1918	Stephen	*Sirdar*	1918	Fairfield
Saladin	1919	Stephen	*Somme*	1918	Fairfield
Sardonyx	1919	Stephen	*Sparrowhawk*	1918	Swan Hunter
Scimitar	1918	Clydebank	*Spear*	1918	Fairfield
Scotsman	1918	Clydebank	*Spindrift*	1919	Fairfield
Scout	1918	Clydebank	*Splendid*	1918	Swan Hunter
Scythe	1918	Clydebank	*Sportive*	1918	Swan Hunter
Seabear	1918	Clydebank	*Stalwart*	1919	Swan Hunter
Seafire	1918	Clydebank	*Steadfast*	1919	Palmers
Searcher	1918	Clydebank	*Sterling*	1919	Palmers
Seawolf	1919	Clydebank	*Stonehenge*	1919	Palmers
Senator	1918	Denny	*Stormcloud*	1919	Palmers
Sepoy	1918	Denny	*Strenuous*	1919	Scotts
Seraph	1918	Denny	*Stronghold*	1919	Scotts
Serapis	1919	Denny	*Sturdy*	1919	Scotts
Serene	1919	Denny	*Success*	1919	Doxford
Sesame	1919	Denny	*Swallow*	1918	Scotts
Shamrock	1919	Doxford	*Swordsman*	1918	Scotts
Shark	1918	Swan Hunter	*Tactician*	1918	Beardmore
Shikari	1924	Doxford, completed by HM Dockyard Chatham	*Tara*	1918	Beardmore
			Tasmania	1919	Beardmore
			Tattoo	1919	Beardmore
Sikh	1918	Fairfield	*Tenedos*	1919	Hawthorn
Simoon	1918	Clydebank	*Thanet*	1919	Hawthorn

UNIT	COMPLETED	BUILDER
Thracian	1922	Hawthorn, completed by HM Dockyard Chatham
Tilbury	1918	Swan Hunter
Tintagel	1918	Swan Hunter
Tribune	1918	White
Trinidad	1918	White
Trojan	1919	White
Truant	1919	White
Trusty	1919	White
Turbulent	1919	Hawthorn

Displacement:	1,075 tons
Length:	276ft
Breadth:	26ft 9in
Draught:	10ft 6in
Armament:	*Main* Three 4in
	Secondary One 2pdr
	Tubes Four 21in (2x2)
	Two 14in either beam at break of forecastle (2x1)
	AS 30 DCs carried.
Machinery:	Turbines on two shafts giving 27,000shp
Max speed:	36kts
Fuel:	250-300 tons oil

Top: HMS *Shikari*, Admiralty 'S' class, at sea in 1925. (R. Perkins)

Bottom: HMS *Tilbury*, Admiralty 'S' class, entering harbour in 1925. (R. Perkins)

CLASS NOTES

This was a coastal design for the North Sea and English Channel; they did, however, travel to far distant seas. They had a long forecastle and tall bridge. The majority of this class had one 14in tube fixed at the break of the forecastle to be launched abeam in night actions. All had two funnels, the foremost broader and taller than the second; both were raked.

HISTORICAL NOTES

HMS *Shikari* on commissioning was the control vessel for the target ships *Agamemnon* and *Centurion*.

HMS *Stalwart*, *Success*, *Swordsman*, *Tattoo* and *Tasmania* were transferred to the Royal Australian Navy in 1918.

HMS *Sterling* was so named due to a typing error; her intended name was *Stirling*.

HMS *Stronghold* on 2 March 1942 was sunk by a Japanese Task Force off the east coast of Malaya.

HMS *Sturdy* was wrecked in bad weather on 30 October 1940, off the Island of Tiree, west Scotland.

HMS *Tenedos* was sunk after Japanese aircraft attack on Colombo Roads on 5 April 1942.

Between 1923 and 1928, both HMS *Thanet* and *Stronghold* were fitted with aircraft catapults on the forecastle.

HMS *Thanet* was sunk by the Japanese on 28 January 1942 off the east coast of Malaya.

HMS *Thracian* was taken by the Japanese whilst beached at Hong Kong in 1942, but was recovered in 1945 and sold in 1947.

YARROW 'S' CLASS

UNIT	COMPLETED
Tomahawk	1918
Torch	1918
Tryphon	1918
Tumult	1918
Turquoise	1919
Tuscan	1919
Tyrian	1919

CLASS NOTES

The characteristics of these ships were as for the Admiralty 'S' class, except that they had a sloping stern and a broader fore funnel.

HISTORICAL NOTES

HMS *Tryphon* grounded off Tenedos on 6 May 1919 but was salvaged and refitted.

Builder:	Yarrow		
Displacement:	930 tons		*Tubes* Four 21in (2x2)
Length:	269ft 6in		AS 30 DCs carried
Breadth:	25ft 9in	**Machinery:**	Turbines on two shafts giving
Draught:	11ft		23,000shp
Armament:	*Main* Three 4in with 30° elevation	**Max speed:**	36kts
	AA One 2pdr	**Fuel:**	215-255 tons oil

HMS *Tuscan*, Yarrow 'S' class, leaving harbour in 1920. (R. Perkins)

HMS *Tyrian*, Yarrow 'S' class, underway in 1925. (R. Perkins)

THORNYCROFT 'S' CLASS

UNIT	COMPLETED
Speedy	1918
Tobago	1918
Torbay	1919
Toreador	1919
Tourmaline	1919

Builder:	Thornycroft
Displacement:	1,087 tons
Length:	27ft 9in
Breadth:	27ft 6in
Draught:	10ft
Armament:	*Main* Three 4in with 30° elevation
	AA Two 2pdr
	Tubes Four 21in (2x2)
	AS 30 DCs carried
Machinery:	Geared turbines on two shafts giving 29,000shp
Max speed:	36kts
Fuel:	250-300 tons oil

Below left: HMS *Toreador*, Thornycroft 'S' class, entering harbour in 1920. (R. Perkins)

Below right: HMS *Tourmaline*, Thornycroft 'S' class, at sea. (R. Perkins)

CLASS NOTES

This class had a greater freeboard than the Yarrow and Admiralty 'S' classes and had two funnels of equal height, taller than the 'S' class. The A gun was mounted on a short shelter deck.

HISTORICAL NOTES

HMS *Tobago*, although not strictly a war loss, was nevertheless a victim of a weapon of war, being mined whilst on patrol in the Black Sea in 1920.

ADMIRALTY 'V' CLASS

UNIT	COMPLETED	BUILDER
Valentine (leader)	1917	Cammell Laird
Valhalla (leader)	1917	Cammell Laird
Valkyrie (leader)	1917	Denny
Valorous (leader)	1917	Denny
Vampire (leader)	1917	White
Vancouver	1918	Beardmore
Vanessa	1918	Beardmore
Vanity	1918	Beardmore
Vanoc	1917	Clydebank
Vanquisher	1917	Clydebank
Vectis	1917	White
Vega	1917	Doxford
Vehement	1917	Denny
Velox	1917	Doxford
Vendetta	1917	Fairfield
Venetia	1917	Fairfield
Venturous	1917	Denny
Verdun	1917	Hawthorn
Versatile	1918	Hawthorn
Verulan	1917	Hawthorn
Vesper	1918	Stephen
Vidette	1918	Stephen
Vimiera	1918	Swan Hunter
Violent	1918	Swan Hunter
Vittoria	1918	Swan Hunter
Vivacious	1917	Yarrow
Vivien	1918	Yarrow
Vortigern	1918	White

Displacement:	1,090 tons
	1,480 tons (full load)
Length:	312ft
Breadth:	29ft 6in
Draught:	10ft 10in
Armament:	*Main* Four 4in (4x1) director controlled
	AA One 3in, One MG
	Tubes Four 21in (2x2)
Machinery:	Geared turbines on two shafts giving
	27,000shp
Max speed:	34kts
Fuel:	320-360 tons oil

known A, B, X and Y positions and superimposed. The AA gun was aft of the second funnel. Some of this class were used as minelayers. HMS *Vampire* had six 21in tubes in two triple mountings.

HISTORICAL NOTES

HMS *Valentine* was beached on the banks of the River Scheldt on 15 May 1940 after aircraft attack.

HMS *Vampire* (RAN) was sunk after surface action with vessels from a Japanese Task Force in the Bay of Bengal on 9 April 1942.

HMS *Vancouver* was renamed *Vimy* on being transferred to Canada in 1928.

HMS *Vehement* was mined and sank in the North Sea on 2 August 1918.

HMS *Venetia* was mined and sank in the Thames Estuary on 19 October 1940.

HMS *Verulam* was mined and sank off Seskaer Island in the Gulf of Finland on the night of 3/4 September 1919.

HMS *Vimiera* was mined and sank off the Nore on 9 January 1942.

HMS *Vittoria* was torpedoed by a Russian Bolshevik submarine in the Gulf of Finland on 1 September 1919

HMS *Vortigern* was torpedoed by an E-boat off the east coast on 14 March 1942.

CLASS NOTES

This class was probably one of the most well known and successful to serve in the Royal Navy. The design was derived in part from the ex-Turkish ships. The 4in guns were mounted in the now well

HMS *Vivacious*, underway leaving harbour flying three White Ensigns and Union flag and pendant numbers; the occasion for this display is not known. (R. Perkins)

HMS *Vampire*, Admiralty 'V' class, at sea in 1921. (R. Perkins)

ADMIRALTY 'W' CLASS

UNIT	COMPLETED	BUILDER
Voyager	1918	Stephen
Wakeful	1917	Beardmore
Walker	1918	Denny
Walpole	1918	Doxford
Walrus	1918	Fairfield
Warwick	1918	Hawthorn
Watchman	1918	Beardmore
Waterhen	1918	Palmers
Wessex	1918	Hawthorn
Westcott	1918	Denny

UNIT	COMPLETED	BUILDER
Westminster	1918	Scotts
Whirlwind	1918	Swan Hunter
Whitley	1918	Doxford
Winchelsea	1918	White
Winchester	1918	White
Windsor	1918	Scotts
Wolfhound	1918	Fairfield
Wrestler	1918	Swan Hunter
Wryneck	1918	Palmers

Displacement:	1,100 tons
Length:	312ft
Breadth:	29ft 6in
Draught:	11ft
Armament:	*Main* Four 4in, director controlled
	Secondary One 3in
	AA One MG
	Tubes Six 21in (2x3)
Machinery:	Geared turbines on two shafts giving 27,000shp
Max speed:	34kts
Fuel:	320-370 tons oil

CLASS NOTES

This class was practically identical to the Admiralty 'V' class apart from having a taller mainmast and slightly greater displacement tonnage.

HISTORICAL NOTES

HMS *Voyager* (RAN) was bombed by Japanese aircraft on 23 September 1942 and beached on Tumor Island.

HMS *Wakeful* sank off Nieuwpoort after being hit by an E-boat torpedo on 29 May 1940.

HMS *Warwick* was torpedoed by U413 off Trevose Head on 20 February 1944.

HMS *Waterhen* whilst manned by the RAN, sank in tow on 30 June 1941 after aircraft attack off Sollom.

HMS *Wessex* sank after aircraft attack on 24 May 1940 near Calais.

HMS *Westcott* was the trials ship for the Hedgehog anti-submarine weapon in 1941.

HMS *Whirlwind* was torpedoed on 5 July 1940 by U34 in the western Mediterranean.

HMS *Whitley* was so named due to a typing error; her intended name was *Whitby*.

HMS *Whitley* was bombed and beached at Nieuwpoort on 19 May 1940.

HMS *Wrestler* was mined and sank off the Normandy Beachhead on 6 June 1944.

HMS *Wryneck* sank after aircraft attack in the Gulf of Nauplia on 27 April 1941.

HMS *Watchman*, Admiralty 'W' class, in 1920. Note minelaying stern. (R. Perkins)

HMS *Wolfhound*, Admiralty 'W' Class at sea about 1939.

THORNYCROFT 'V' AND 'W' CLASS

Units:	*Viceroy, Wolsey, Woolston*
Completed:	1918
Builder:	Thornycroft
Displacement:	1,120 tons
Length:	312ft
Breadth:	30ft 6in
Draught:	10ft 6in
Armament:	*Main* Three 4in, director controlled
	AA One 3in, One MG
	Tubes Six 21in (2x3)
Machinery:	Geared turbines on two shafts giving 30,000shp
Max speed:	35kts
Fuel:	320-370 tons oil

HMS *Viscount*, Thornycroft 'V & W' class, at anchor in 1920. (R. Perkins)

CLASS NOTES

Although the four ships in this class had slightly more freeboard, and taller and broader after funnels, they were very similar to the 'V' and 'W' classes of Admiralty design. On deep-load draught, their speed was the same, namely 31kts. This class had a shorter main mast than any other 'V' class destroyer.

HMS *Viceroy* and *Viscount* had four 21in tubes in twin mountings.

HMS *Wolsey*, Thornycroft 'V & W' class, at anchor in 1920. (R. Perkins)

EX-PROVISIONAL RUSSIAN GOVERNMENT

Unit:	Derski
Completed:	1913
Displacement:	1,100 tons
Length:	308ft
Breadth:	29ft 6in
Draught:	9ft
Armament:	*Main* Three 4in (3x1)
	AA One 9pdr
	Tubes Ten 17.7in (5x2)
Machinery:	Turbines on two shafts giving 25,500shp
Max speed:	34kts
Fuel:	255-280 tons oil

CLASS NOTES

The *Derski* was quite a modern torpedo boat destroyer and is understood to have been built to a British design. She was taken over by the Royal Navy after the fall of Kerensky's Government until transfer was effected to the naval force attached to General Denikin.

THORNYCROFT MODIFIED 'W' CLASS

Units:	Wishart, Witch
Commenced:	1918
Completed:	Wishart 1920, Witch 1924
Builder:	Thornycroft
Displacement:	1,140 tons
	1,550 tons (full load)
Length:	312ft
Breadth:	30ft
Draught:	11ft
Armament:	*Main* Four 4.7in, director controlled
	AA One 3in, One MG
	Tubes Six 21in (2x3)
Machinery:	Geared turbines on two shafts giving 30,000shp

Max speed:	32kts
Fuel:	320-375 tons oil

CLASS NOTES

With the exception of the staggered 2pdr mountings and the taller and broader fore funnel, there was very little difference between this class and the Thornycroft 'V' and 'W' class.

HMS *Wishart* had only three tubes.

HMS *Witch*, although built and launched at Thornycrofts, was fitted out and completed at HM Dockyard Devonport.

HMS *Wishart*, Thornycroft modified 'W' class, at anchor in 1937. (R. Perkins)

HMS *Witch*, Thornycroft modified 'W' class, entering harbour in 1924.

ADMIRALTY MODIFIED 'W' CLASS

UNIT	COMPLETED	BUILDER
Vansittart	1920	Beardmore
Venomous (ex-Venom)	1919	Clydebank
Verity	1920	Clydebank
Veteran	1919	Clydebank
Vimy (ex-Vantage; later HMCS Vancouver)	1919	Beardmore
Volunteer	1919	Denny
Wanderer	1919	Fairfield
Whitehall	1920	Swan-Hunter*
Whitshed	1919	Swan-Hunter
Wild Swan	1919	Swan-Hunter
Witherington	1919	White
Wivern	1919	White
Wolverine	1920	White
Worcester	1922	White+
Wren	1919	Yarrow++
Wye	1919	Yarrow+++

*Completed by HM Dockyard, Chatham.
+Completed by HM Dockyard, Portsmouth.
++Completed by HM Dockyard, Pembroke.
+++ Cancelled September 1919.

Displacement:	1,120 tons, 1,500 tons (full load)
Length:	312ft
Breadth:	29ft 6in
Draught:	11ft
Armament:	*Main* Four 4.7 (4x1in shields)
	AA Two 2pdr
	Tubes Six 21in (2x3)
Machinery:	Geared turbines on two shafts giving 27,000shp
Max speed:	34kts
Fuel:	320-375 tons oil

All of this class had director control for the main armament. After the completion of this class in 1922, no other destroyers were launched until 1926.

CLASS NOTES

Seven of this class had the same funnel arrangement as the 'V' class and seven as the 'W' class. The 2-pounder guns were staggered aft of the second funnel. A very successful type with good service in the Second World War.

HISTORICAL NOTES

HMS *Wild Swan* sank on 17 June 1942 following an aircraft attack and later collision with a Spanish trawler – 100 miles west of the French coast.

HMS *Wren* sank after aircraft attack off the east coast of Aldeburgh on 27 July 1940.

HMS *Veteran* was torpedoed by U404 in the western Atlantic on 28 September 1942.

HMS *Worcester* was mined and severely damaged on 23 December 1943 in the North Sea but made port and was used as the accommodation ship *Yeoman*.

HMS *Whitshed*, Admiralty modified 'W' class, leaving harbour in 1941. (MoD (Navy))

HMS *Worcester*, Admiralty modified 'W' class, moored and flying a masthead pendant similar to the two destroyers in the background. (IWM)

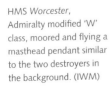

HMS *Wren* in rough seas. (Charles E. Brown)

ADMIRALTY LARGE DESIGN

UNIT	COMPLETED
Bruce	1918
Campbell	1918
Douglas	1918
Mackay	1919
Malcolm	1919
Montrose	1918
Scott	1917
Stuart	1918

Builder:	Cammell Laird (*Montrose* and *Stuart* Hawthorn Leslie)
Displacement:	1,801 tons
Length:	322ft 6in
Breadth:	31ft 9in
Draught:	12ft 6in
Armament:	*Main* Five 4.7in
	Secondary One 3in AA
	AA Two 2pdr, one MG
	Tubes Six 21in (2x3)
Machinery:	Geared turbines on two shafts giving 40,000shp
Max speed:	36.5kts
Fuel:	400-500 tons oil

CLASS NOTES

In this class, both funnels were of the same height and were circular. *Barrington* and *Hughes*, both building at Cammell Laird, were cancelled in 1918. Of a similar design to, but slightly larger than, the Thornycroft leaders ordered under the Emergency War Programme 1916–18, all of this class were built as leaders.

HISTORICAL NOTES

HMS *Bruce* was expended as a target on 22 November 1939 off the Isle of Wight.

HMS *Scott* was torpedoed on 15 August 1918 by UC17 in the North Sea off the Danish coast.

Opposite above: HMS *Douglas*, Admiralty large design, anchored in 1924. (R. Perkins)

Opposite below: HMS *Mackay*, Admiralty large design, at sea in 1919. (R. Perkins)

THORNYCROFT TYPE

UNIT	COMPLETED
Broke (ex-*Rooke*)	1920
Keppel	1921
Shakespeare	1917
Spenser	1917
Wallace	1919

Builder:	Thornycroft
Displacement:	1,480 tons
Length:	329ft
Breadth:	31ft 9in
Draught:	12ft 6in
Armament:	*Main* Five 4.7in, director controlled
	Secondary One 3in DP
	AA Two 2pdr, one MG
	Tubes Six 21in (2x3)
Machinery:	Geared turbines on two shafts giving 40,000shp
Max speed:	36kts
Fuel:	400–500 tons oil

CLASS NOTES

This class, all of which were leaders, was similar in design to the Admiralty leaders of the previous class. *Saunders* and *Spragge* of this class, building at Thornycroft, were cancelled 1918. *Broke* was completed at HM Dockyard, *Pembroke* and *Keppel* at Portsmouth.

HISTORICAL NOTES

HMS *Broke* took part in a direct assault on Algiers Harbour during Operation Torch on 8 November 1942, and in the best traditions cut through the boom and berthed safely alongside to land the troops she was carrying. Unfortunately, she sustained severe hits from the Vichy French batteries and sank the following day.

Top: HMS *Keppel*, Thornycroft Type, anchored in 1939. (R. Perkins)

Above: HMS *Broke*, Thornycroft Type, at sea in 1920.

THORNYCROFT EXPERIMENTAL 'A' CLASS

Unit:	Amazon
Commenced:	1925
Completed:	1926
Builders:	Thornycroft
Displacement:	1,350 tons
Length:	31ft 9in PP
Breadth:	31ft 6in
Draught:	9ft 6in
Armament:	*Main* Four 4.7in
	Secondary Five .5in MG
	AA One 3in
	Tubes Six 21in (2x3)
Machinery:	Geared turbines on two shafts giving 39,500shp
Max speed:	37kts
Fuel:	433 tons oil

CLASS NOTES

HMS *Amazon* was Thornycroft's answer to the Admiralty's request for a destroyer design embodying all lessons learned during the war, and she was built under the 1924–25 estimate. She was fitted with Parsons low-pressure turbines for cruising and was designed for home and tropical use with high freeboard and improved accommodation.

HMS *Amazon*, Thornycroft experimental 'A' class, at sea in 1926.

YARROW EXPERIMENTAL 'A' CLASS

Unit:	Ambuscade
Commenced:	1924
Completed:	1926
Builders:	Yarrow
Displacement:	1,170 tons
Length:	307ft PP
Breadth:	31ft
Draught:	8ft 3in
Armament:	Main Four 4.7in
	Secondary Five .5in MG
	AA One 3in
	Tubes Three 21in (1x3)
Machinery:	Geared turbines on two shafts giving 33,000shp
Max speed:	35kts
Fuel:	385 tons oil

CLASS NOTES

HMS *Ambuscade* was Yarrow's answer to the Admiralty's request for a destroyer design, embodying all lessons learned during the war, and was built under the 1924–25 estimate. She was fitted with Parsons low-pressure turbines for cruising and was designed for home and tropical use with high freeboard and improved accommodation.

HMS *Ambuscade*, Thornycroft experimental 'A' class, 1943. Note Squid in A position and radar above bridge. (MoD (Navy))

'A' CLASS   The leader of this Class was HMS *CODRINGTON*

UNIT	BUILDER
Acasta	Clydebank
Achates	Clydebank
Acheron	Thornycroft
Active	Hawthorn Leslie
Antelope	Hawthorn Leslie
Anthony	Scotts SB
Ardent	Scotts SB
Arrow	Vickers Armstrong (Barrow)
Keith (leader)	Vickers Armstrong (Barrow)

Commenced:	1928 (Keith 1929)
Completed:	1930 (Acheron and Keith 1931)
Displacement:	1,375 tons (Keith 1,400 tons)
Length:	323ft
Breadth:	32ft 9in (Keith 32ft 3in)
Draught:	8ft 6in
Armament:	Main Four 4.7in
	AA Two 2pdr, five MG
	Tubes Eight 21in (2x4)
Machinery:	Geared turbines on two shafts giving 34,000shp
Max speed:	35.25kts (Keith 34.25kts)
Fuel:	380 tons oil (Keith 470)

HMS *Keith*, leader of the new 'A' class, at sea. (Vickers)

CLASS NOTES

This was the first full class to mount quadruple tubes. All ships easily passed their acceptance trials, and proved to be economical vessels. All of this class were fitted for high speed minesweeping (HSMS).

HISTORICAL NOTES

HMS *Acasta* took part in the action with the *Scharnhorst* and *Gneisenau*, and sank from shellfire on 8 June 1940.

HMS *Achates* foundered after heavy weather, following shellfire from the *Admiral Hipper* in the Barents Sea on 31 December 1942.

HMS *Acheron* sank after she was mined in the English Channel, south of the Isle of Wight, on 8 December 1940.

HMS *Ardent* took part in the action with the *Scharnhorst* and *Gneisenau*, and sank from shellfire on 8 June 1940.

HMS *Arrow* was severly damaged when the SS *Port le Monte Algiers* exploded on 4 August 1943 and became a total loss.

HMS *Keith* sank after aircraft attack off Dunkirk on 1 June 1940.

'B' CLASS   The leader of this Class was HMS *KEITH*

UNIT	BUILDER
Basilisk	Clydebank
Beagle	Clydebank
Blanche	Hawthorne-Leslie
Boadicea	Hawthorne-Leslie
Boreas	Palmers
Brazen	Palmers
Brilliant	Swan Hunter
Bulldog	Swan Hunter
Kempenfelt (leader)	White

Commenced:	1929 (*Kempenfelt* 1930)
Completed:	1931
Displacement:	1,360 tons (*Kempenfelt* 1,390 tons)
Length:	323ft (*Kempenfelt* 326ft)
Breadth:	32ft 3in (*Kempenfelt* 33ft)
Draught:	8ft 6in (*Kempenfelt* 8ft 8in)
Armament:	Main Four 4.7in
	AA Two 2pdr, five MG
	Tubes Eight 21in (2x4)
Machinery:	Geared turbines on two shafts giving 34,000shp (*Kempenfelt* 36,000shp)

Max speed:	34kts
Fuel:	380 tons oil (*Kempenfelt* 470)

CLASS NOTES

All this class were very similar to the new 'A' class and were good economical ships.

HISTORICAL NOTES

HMS *Basilisk* sank after aircraft attack off Dunkirk on 1 June 1940.

HMS *Blanche* was the first destroyer to be sunk in the Second World War, this occurring on 13 November 1939 when she was mined in the Thames Estuary.

HMS *Boadicea* sank after aircraft attack off Portland on 13 June 1944.

HMS *Brazen* sank whilst in tow after aircraft attack off Dover on 20 July 1940.

HMS *Boadicea*, new 'B' class, at anchor in 1925. (R. Perkins)

HMS *Bulldog*, new 'B' class, 1944. Note A and Y guns suppressed with radar, HF, MF, DF aerials on mainmast. (MoD (Navy))

'C' CLASS   The leader of this Class was HMS *KEMPENFELT* (later HMCS *ASSINIBOINE*)

Units:	*Comet, Crescent, Crusader, Cygnet*
Commenced:	1930
Completed:	1932
Builders:	Vickers Armstrong (Barrow) (*Crescent, Cygnet*), HM Dockyard Portsmouth (*Crusader, Comet*)
Displacement:	1,375 tons
Length:	326ft
Breadth:	33ft
Draught:	8ft 6in
Armament:	*Main* Four 4.7in
	Secondary Seven smaller
	Tubes Eight 21in (2x4)
Machinery:	Geared turbines on two shafts giving 36,000shp
Max speed:	36kts
Fuel:	470 tons oil

CLASS NOTES

General arrangement as the new 'D' class. The destroyers were transferred to the Royal Canadian Navy in 1937.

HISTORICAL NOTES

HMCS *Fraser* (ex-*Crescent*) sank after collision with HMS *Calcutta* in the River Gironde on 28 June 1940.

HMCS *Ottawa* (ex-*Crusader*) was torpedoed by U91 in the Gulf of St Lawrence on 14 September 1942.

HMS *Crescent*, new 'C' class, at sea. Note HSMS gear on the stern. (Vickers)

HMS *Crusader*, new 'C' class, at anchor in 1927. Note detail of bridge director and searchlight on bandstand between the tubes; HSMS gear on the stern. (R. Perkins)

ADMIRALTY LEADER *CODRINGTON*

Unit:	*Codrington*	Draught:	12ft 3in
Commenced:	1928	Armament:	*Main* Five 4.7in
Completed:	1930		*AA* Two 2pdr, five MGs
Builder:	Swan Hunter		*Tubes* Eight 21in (2x4)
Displacement:	1,540 tons	Machinery:	Geared turbines on two shafts giving
	2,000 tons (full load)		39,000shp
Length:	332ft	Max speed:	35kts
Breadth:	33 ft 9in	Fuel:	500 tons oil

HMS *Codrington*, Admiralty leader, at a mooring in 1935. (R. Perkins)

CLASS NOTES

HMS *Codrington* attained the speed of 40kts on trials and in 1930 represented the ultimate in destroyer design; she was built under the 1928 programme.

HISTORICAL NOTES

HMS *Codrington* was named to honour the centenary of the Battle of Navarino in 1827 at which Admiral Sir Edward Codrington was the Naval Commander in Chief.

HMS *Codrington* steamed from Scapa Flow to Dover, over 530 miles in under 24 hours, in 1940. She saw service off the Netherlands and at Dunkirk and took on at least 2,000 men of the British Expeditionary Force. After the Norwegian Campaign the same year she was sunk by aircraft attack whilst in Dover Harbour on 27 July 1940.

'D' CLASS

UNIT	COMPLETED	BUILDER
Dainty	1933	Fairfield
Daring	1932	Thornycroft
Decoy	1933	Thornycroft
Defender	1932	Vickers Armstrong (Barrow)
Delight	1933	Fairfield
Diamond	1932	Vickers Armstrong (Barrow)
Diana	1932	Palmers
Duchess	1933	Palmers
Duncan	1933	HM Dockyard Portsmouth (leader)

Commenced:	1931
Displacement:	1,375 tons (*Duncan* 1,400)
Length:	326ft
Breadth:	33ft (*Duncan* 33ft 9in)
Draught:	8ft 6in
Armament:	*Main* Four 4.7in
	Secondary Six smaller
	Tubes Eight 21in (2x4)
Machinery:	Geared turbines on two shafts giving 36,000shp (38,000shp in *Duncan*)
Max speed:	36kts (*Duncan* 36.75kts)
Fuel:	470 tons oil

CLASS NOTES

HMS *Duncan* had crow's nests and a slightly different-shaped bridge which included provision for a radar cabin.

HISTORICAL NOTES

HMS *Dainty* sank after aircraft attack off Tobruk on 24 February 1941.

HMS *Daring* was torpedoed by U23 in the North Sea off Duncansby Head on 18 February 1940.

HMS *Decoy* later became HMCS *Kootenay*.

HMS *Defender* sank after air attack off Tobruk on 12 July 1941.

HMS *Delight* sank after aircraft attack off Dover on 29 July 1940.

HMS *Diamond* sank after aircraft attack in the Gulf of Nauplia on 27 April 1941.

HMS *Duchess* foundered after collision with HMS *Barham* off the west Scottish coast on 13 December 1939.

HMCS *Margaree* (ex-*Diana*) sank after collision with SS *Port Fairy* in the North Atlantic on 22 October 1940.

HMS *Diamond*, 'D' class, at sea on builder's trials in 1932. Note galley-type funnels on port side of B gun blast shield and attached to the forward funnel. (Vickers)

HMS *Defender*, 'D' class, on builder's trials off Walney Island. (Vickers)

'E' CLASS

UNIT	BUILDER
Echo	Denny
Eclipse	Denny
Electra	Hawthorn Leslie
Encounter	Hawthorn Leslie
Escapade	Scotts SB
Escort	Scotts SB
Esk	Swan-Hunter
Exmouth (leader)	HM Dockyard Portsmouth
Express	Swan Hunter

Commenced:	1933
Completed:	1934
Displacement:	1,350 tons (*Escapade* 1,375 tons)
Length:	329ft (*Exmouth* 343ft)
Breadth:	33ft 3in (*Exmouth* 33ft 9in)
Draught:	8ft 6in (*Exmouth* 8ft 8in)
Armament:	*Main* Four 4.7in
	AA Six smaller
	Tubes Eight 21in (2x4)
Machinery:	Geared turbines on two shafts giving 36,000shp (*Exmouth* 38,000shp)
Max speed:	36kts (*Exmouth* 36.75kts)
Fuel:	490 tons oil (*Exmouth*)
Range:	6,000 miles at 15kts

CLASS NOTES

Both of the leaders of this class and the 'F' class had a third 4.7in gun mounted on a deck house between the funnels, giving HMS *Exmouth* five 4.7in guns. HMS *Esk* and *Express* were equipped as minelayers and had a tripod main mast.

HISTORICAL NOTES

HMS *Echo* later became RHN *Navarinon*.

HMS *Eclipse* sank after she was mined in the Aegean, east of Kalyminos, on 23 October 1943.

HMS *Electra* sank in action with Japanese surface vessels (including HIM *Jintsu*) in the Battle of the Java Sea on 27 February 1942.

HMS *Encounter* sank in action with Japanese cruisers HIM *Ashigara* and *Myoko* on 1 March 1942.

HMS *Escort* sank in two after being torpedoed by Italian U-boat *Marconi* in the western Mediterranean on 11 July 1940.

HMS *Esk* sank after she was mined in the Moray Firth on 21 January 1940.

HMS *Exmouth* sank after being torpedoed by U22 in the Moray Firth on 21 January 1941.

HMS *Express* later became HMCS *Gatineau*.

HMS *Encounter*, 'E' class, at anchor in 1937. (R. Perkins)

HMS *Escapade*, 'E' class, 1945. Note A position Squid deleted by censor and Y gun suppressed. (MoD (Navy))

'F' CLASS

UNIT	BUILDER
Fame	Vickers Armstrong (Tyne)
Faulknor (leader)	Yarrow
Fearless	Cammell Laird
Firedrake	Vickers Armstrong (Tyne)
Foresight	Cammell Laird
Forester	White
Fortune	Clydebank
Foxhound	Clydebank
Fury	White

Commenced:	1933
Completed:	1935
Displacement:	1,360 tons (*Faulknor* 1,460 tons)
Length:	329ft 6in (*Faulknor* 340ft wl)
Breadth:	33ft 3in (*Faulknor* 33ft 9in)
Draught:	8ft 6in (*Faulknor* 8ft 6in)
Armament:	*Main* Four 4.7in (*Faulknor* Five)
	AA Six smaller
	Tubes Eight 21in (2x4)
Machinery:	Geared turbines on two shafts giving 36,000shp (*Faulknor* 38,000shp)
Fuel:	490 tons oil
Range:	6,000 miles at 15kts (average)

HMS *Fame*, 'F' class, entering harbour in 1943. (MoD (Navy))

HMS *Forester*, 'F' class, on Atlantic convoy duty in 1942. (IWM)

CLASS NOTES

This was virtually a repeat of the 1934 'E' class.

HISTORICAL NOTES

HMS *Fearless* sank after being struck by an aircraft-launched torpedo whilst on convoy escort in the Mediterranean on 23 July 1941.

HMS *Firedrake* was torpedoed by U211 in the western Atlantic on 17 December 1942.

HMS *Foresight* was struck by an aircraft-launched torpedo and not being salvageable was despatched by own forces on 12 August 1942.

HMS *Fortune* later became HMCS *Saskatchewan*.

HMS *Foxhound* later became HMCS *Qu'Appelle*.

HMS *Fury* was mined and was damaged beyond repair off the Normandy beachhead on 21 June 1944.

'G' CLASS

UNIT	BUILDER
Gallant	Stephen
Garland	Fairfield
Gipsy	Fairfield
Glowworm	Thornycroft
Grafton	Thornycroft
Grenade	Stephen
Grenville (leader)	Yarrow
Greyhound	Vickers Armstrong (Barrow)
Griffin	Vickers Armstrong (Barrow)

Commenced:	1934
Completed:	1936
Displacement:	1,335 tons (*Grenville* 1,485 tons)
Length:	323ft (*Grenville* 327ft wl)
Breadth:	34ft 6in
Draught:	8ft 3in (*Grenville* 8ft 8in)
Armament:	*Main* Four 4.7in (*Grenville* Five)
	AA Six smaller
	Tubes Eight 21in (2x4)
Machinery:	Geared turbines on two shafts giving 34,000shp (*Grenville* 38,000shp)
Max speed:	36kts (*Grenville* 36.5kts)
Fuel:	455 tons oil (*Grenville* 475)

CLASS NOTES

All this class had tripod main masts and were very similar to the following 'H' class. HMS *Glowworm* was 1,345 tons displacement and had quintuple tubes (10.21in). She was the trials vessel for the quintuple torpedo tube mounting.

HISTORICAL NOTES

HMS *Garland* was transferred to Poland in 1940.

HMS *Gallant* was hit by aircraft torpedoes on 10 June 1941 but proceeded to Grand Harbour, Malta. She sank after a further bombing attack on 20 June 1941.

HMS *Gipsy* was mined and sank off Harwich on 21 November 1939.

HMS *Glowworm*, after running short of ammunition, rammed and damaged the *Admiral Hipper* but was lost on 8 April 1940.

HMS *Grafton* was torpedoed by an E-boat and sank off Dunkirk on 29 May 1940.

HMS *Grenade* sank after aircraft attack off Dunkirk on 29 May 1940.

HMS *Grenville* was mined and sank in the North Sea on 20 January 1940.

HMS *Greyhound* sank after aircraft attack off Crete on 22 May 1941.

HMS *Griffin* later became HMCS *Ottawa*.

HMS *Glowworm*, 'G' class, at anchor in 1937. (R. Perkins)

HMS *Grafton*, 'G' class, at anchor in 1937. (R. Perkins)

HMS *Griffin* at sea with HSMS gear on her stern and Y gun suppressed. (Vickers)

'H' CLASS

UNIT	BUILDER
Hardy (leader)	Cammell Laird
Hasty	Denny
Havock	Denny
Hereward	Vickers Armstrong (Tyne)
Hero	Vickers Armstrong (Tyne)
Hostile	Scotts SB
Hotspur	Scotts SB
Hunter	Swan Hunter
Hyperion	Swan Hunter

Commenced:	1935
Completed:	1936 (*Havock* 1937)
Displacement:	1,340 tons (*Hardy* 1,505 tons)
Length:	323ft (*Hardy* 334ft)
Breadth:	33ft (*Hardy* 34ft)
Draught:	8ft 6in (*Hardy* 8ft 8in)
Armament:	*Main* Four 4.7in (*Hardy* Five)
	AA Six smaller
	Tubes Eight 21in (2x4)
Machinery:	Geared turbines on two shafts giving 34,000shp (*Hardy* 38,000shp)
Max speed:	36kts (*Hardy* 36.75kts)
Fuel:	455 tons oil (*Hardy* 475)

CLASS NOTES
Of very similar design to the 'G' class, HMS *Hero* had shorter funnels and a more streamlined bridge. HMS *Hereward* was the trials vessel for the twin 4.7in mounting for the 'Tribal' class.

HISTORICAL NOTES

HMS *Hardy* (1936) foundered on 10 April 1940 after action with German destroyers Z2 and Z11 in the Battle of Narvik.

HMS *Hasty* sank on 15 June 1942 after aircraft attack whilst escorting a Mediterranean convoy, being despatched by HMS *Hotspur*.

HMS *Havock* was wrecked on the Tunisian coast near Kelibia on 6 April 1942.

HMS *Hereward* sank on 29 May 1941 after aircraft attack off Crete.

HMS *Hero* later became HMCS *Chaudiere*.

HMS *Hostile* was mined and sank off Malta on 23 August 1940.

HMS *Hunter* sank after action with German destroyers Z2 and Z11, and collision with HMS *Hotspur* at Narvik, 10 April 1940.

HMS *Hyperion* was mined laid by the Italian U-boat *Serpente* on 22 December 1940 off Pantellaria and was later sunk by HMS *Ilex*.

HMS *Hurricane*, 'H' class, leaving Barrow after commissioning. The differences between the Brazilian (see page 86) and British 'H' classes are apparent – altered bridge superstructure and armament. (Vickers)

HMS *Hotspur*, 'H' class, at a mooring in 1943. (MoD (Navy))

'I' CLASS

UNIT	BUILDER
Icarus	Clydebank
Ilex	Clydebank
Imogen	Hawthorn Leslie
Imperial	Hawthorn Leslie
Impulsive	White
Inglefield (leader)	Cammell Laird
Intrepid	White
Isis	Yarrow
Ivanhoe	Yarrow

Commenced:	1936
Completed:	1937 (*Impulsive* 1938)
Displacement:	1,370 tons (*Inglefield* 1,530 tons)
Length:	320ft (*Inglefield* 334ft wl)
Breadth:	33ft (*Inglefield* 34ft)
Draught:	8ft 6in (*Inglefield* 8ft 8in)
Armament:	*Main* Four 4.7in (*Inglefield* Five)
	AA Six smaller
	Tubes Ten 21in (2x5)
Machinery:	Geared turbines on two shafts giving 34,000shp (*Inglefield* 38,000shp)
Max speed:	36kts (*Inglefield* 36.5kts)
Fuel:	455 tons oil (*Inglefield* 470)

CLASS NOTES
All the ships in this class fitted for HSMS.

HISTORICAL NOTES
HMS *Imogen* sank on 16 July 1940 after colliding in fog in the Pentland Firth with HMS *Glasgow*.

HMS *Imperial* was attacked by enemy aircraft off Crete on 29 May 1941. Disabled, she was later sunk by HMS *Hotspur*.

HMS *Inglefield* was hit by a glider bomb launched by an enemy aircraft and later sank off the Anzio beachhead on 25 February 1944.

HMS *Intrepid* sank after aircraft attack in the Aegean on 26 September 1943.

HMS *Isis* was mined and sank off Normandy on 20 July 1944.

HMS *Ivanhoe* was mined on 1 September 1940 and sank in the mouth of the River Texel.

Below left: HMS *Imperial*, 'I' class, leaving harbour in 1937. (R. Perkins)

Below: HMS *Intrepid*, 'I' class, without guns and flying builder's flag in 1937. (R. Perkins)

'TRIBAL' CLASS

UNIT	COMPLETED	BUILDER	UNIT	COMPLETED	BUILDER
Afridi (leader)	1938	Vickers Armstrong (Tyne)	*Mashona*	1939	Vickers Armstrong (Tyne)
Ashanti	1938	Denny	*Matebele*	1939	Scotts SB
Bedouin	1939	Denny	*Mohawk*	1938	Thornycroft
Cossack (leader)	1938	Vickers Armstrong (Tyne)	*Nubian*	1938	Thornycroft
Eskimo	1938	Vickers Armstrong (Tyne)	*Punjabi*	1939	Scotts SB
			Sikh	1938	Stephen
Gurkha	1938	Fairfield	*Somali* (leader)	1938	Swan Hunter
Maori	1939	Fairfield	*Tartar* (leader)	1939	Swan Hunter
			Zulu	1938	Stephen

Commenced:	1936 (*Bedouin* 1937)
Displacement:	1,870 tons
	2,520 tons (full load)
Length:	355ft 6in
Breadth:	36ft 6in
Draught:	9ft
Armament:	*Main* Eight 4.7in (4x2in shields)
	AA Six smaller
	Tubes Four 21in (1x4)
Machinery:	Geared turbines on two shafts giving 44,000shp
Max speed:	36.5kts
Fuel:	520 tons oil

CLASS NOTES

The leaders were of similar appearance to the remainder. The 'Tribal' class of 1936 were the first Royal Naval destroyers to have their main armament in twin mountings. Both masts were tripod and these destroyers were the largest in tonnage since HMS *Codrington* of 1930. HMS *Larne* was renamed *Gurkha* in 1940, see 'Lightning' class.

HISTORICAL NOTES

HMS *Afridi* sank on 3 May 1940 after aircraft attack off the coast of Norway.

HMS *Bedouin* was hit by an aircraft-launched torpedo on 15 June 1942 and later sunk by gunfire of own forces in the central Mediterranean.

HMS *Cossack* was torpedoed by U563 and/or U1997 off Gibraltar on 27 October 1941.

HMS *Gurkha* was severely damaged by aircraft attack on 8 April 1940 and foundered off Bergen.

HMS *Maori* sank on 12 February 1942 after aircraft attack off Malta.

HMS *Mashona* sank on 28 May 1941 after aircraft attack off the west coast of Ireland.

HMS *Matabele* was torpedoed by U454 on 17 January 1942 off the North Cape.

HMS *Mohawk* was torpedoed by the Italian destroyer *Tarigo* on 16 April 1941 off Cape Bon.

HMS *Punjabi* sank after collision with HMS *King George V* in the Western Approaches on 8 May 1942.

HMS *Sikh* sank on 14 September 1942 after engaging enemy shore batteries at Tobruk.

HMS *Somali* sank in two on 8 September 1942, three days after being torpedoed by enemy aircraft off the North Cape.

HMS *Zulu* whilst engaging shore batteries at Tobruk suffered severe damage and sank on 14 September 1942.

HMS *Ashanti*, 'Tribal' class. Note twin 4.7in X mounting suppressed, and twin 4in DP/HA/AA mounting substituted. (IWM)

HMS *Bedouin*, 'Tribal' class, in Narvik Fjord 1940. Note X mounting twin 4.7in suppressed and twin 4in DP/HA/AA mounting substituted. (IWM)

'JAVELIN' CLASS

J GROUP

UNIT	BUILDER
Jackal	Clydebank
Jaguar	Denny
Janus	Swan Hunter
Javelin (ex-*Kashmir*)	Clydebank
Jersey	White
Jupiter	Yarrow
Juno (ex-*Jamaica*)	Fairfield
Jervis (leader)	Hawthorn Leslie

Commenced:	1937
Completed:	1939
Displacement:	1,690 tons (*Jervis* 1,695 tons)
Length:	348ft
Breadth:	35ft
Draught:	9ft
Armament:	*Main* Six 4.7in (3x2in shields)
	AA Six smaller
	Tubes Ten 21in (2x5)
Machinery:	Geared turbines on two shafts giving 40,000shp
Max speed:	36kts
Fuel:	485 tons oil

CLASS NOTES

The three groups of this class were based on the best points of the 'Intrepid' and 'Tribal' classes and were the first one-funnel destroyer class since the 'A' class in 1895 which had *Zephyr* and *Fervent* with one funnel each. It was intended that this class would consist of eight private ships and one leader, but *Jubilant* was cancelled after the decision to build classes of eight was reached. She would have been built by White.

HISTORICAL NOTES

HMS *Jackal* sank on 11 May 1942 after aircraft attack in the eastern Mediterranean.

HMS *Jaguar* was torpedoed by U652 off the coast of Libya on 26 March 1942.

HMS *Janus* whilst supporting the Pontine Landing sank after aircraft attack on 23 June 1944.

HMS *Jersey* was mined and sank in the entrance to Grand Harbour, Malta on 2 May 1941.

HMS *Juno* sank on 20 May 1941 after aircraft attack off Crete.

HMS *Jupiter* attacked and sank the Japanese submarine 160 on 17 January 1942 25 miles off Krakatoa, then on 27 February 1942 was torpedoed during the Battle of the Java Sea.

HMS *Javelin*, 'Javelin' class J group, at anchor in 1941. Note no radar and enveloping gunshields. (MoD (Navy))

HMS *Jervis*, 'Javelin' class J group, entering harbour in 1945. (MoD (Navy))

K GROUP

UNIT	BUILDER		UNIT	BUILDER
Khandahar	Denny		*Khartoum*	Swan Hunter
Kashmir (ex-*Javelin*)	Thornycroft		*Kimberley*	Thornycroft
Kelly (leader)	Hawthorn Leslie		*Kingston*	White
Kelvin	Fairfield		*Kipling*	Yarrow

Commenced:	1937 (*Khandahar* and *Kimberley* 1938)
Displacement:	1,690 tons
	(*Kelly* 1,695 tons)
Length:	348ft
Breadth:	35ft
Draught:	9ft
Armament:	*Main* Six 4.7in (3x2)
	AA Six smaller
	Tubes Ten 21in (2x5)
Machinery:	Geared turbines on two shafts giving 40,000shp
Max speed:	36kts
Fuel:	485 tons oil

CLASS NOTES

All built to the same design as the 'J' group.

HISTORICAL NOTES

HMS *Khandahar* was mined on 19 December 1941 off the coast of Libya and sank on 20 December 1941.

HMS *Kashmir* sank after aircraft attack off Crete on 22 May 1941.

HMS *Kelly* sank after aircraft attack off Crete on 23 May 1941.

HMS *Khartoum* on 23 June 1940 was on patrol off Perim when the air vessel of the starboard torpedo mounting exploded causing an uncontrollable fire, necessitating beaching the ship and abandonment.

HMS *Kingston* was hit on 11 April 1942 in a bombing raid on Valletta Harbour and destroyed.

HMS *Kipling* sank after aircraft attack in the eastern Mediterranean on 11 May 1942.

HMS *Kelly*, 'Javelin' class K group, on trials. (Swan Hunter)

N GROUP

UNIT	BUILDER
Napier (leader)	Fairfield
Nerissa	John Brown
Nestor	Fairfield
Nizam	John Brown
Noble (ex-*Nerissa*)	John Brown
Nonpareil	Denny
Norman	Thornycroft
Norseman	Thornycroft

Commenced:	1939
Completed:	1941 (*Nerissa* and *Napier* 1940)
Displacement:	1,690 tons (*Napier* 1,695 tons)
Length:	348ft
Breadth:	35ft
Draught:	9ft
Armament:	*Main* Six 4.7in (3x2)
	AA Four 40mm
	Six 20mm
	Tubes Ten 21in (2x5)
	AS 30 DCs carried
Machinery:	Geared turbines on two shafts giving 40,000shp
Max speed:	36kts
Fuel:	500 tons oil

CLASS NOTES

HMS *Noble* and *Nonpareil* were the second of the name in this class, the earlier constructions having been sold to the Netherlands. A number of this class were completed with a 4in gun in place of the after tubes. All ships had improved AA firepower.

HISTORICAL NOTES

HMS *Nerissa* was transferred to Poland as *Piorun*.

HMS *Nestor* (whilst under RAN) sank after aircraft attack on 15 June 1942 escorting a Malta convoy.

HMS *Norseman* was renamed *Nepal* in recognition of services by that kingdom to the war effort.

HMS *Nizam*, 'Javelin' class N group, at sea. (MoD (Navy))

'LIGHTNING' CLASS

L GROUP

UNIT	BUILDER
Laforey (leader)	Yarrow
Lance	Yarrow
Larne (later *Gurkha* (2))	Cammell Laird
Legion	Hawthorn Leslie
Lightning	Hawthorn Leslie
Lively	Cammell Laird
Lookout	Scotts SB
Loyal	Scotts SB

CLASS NOTES

The Y 4in guns were on the same deckhouse as those in the X position. The 4.7in had 45° elevation, the 4in being AA weapons with 80° elevations. The 4.7in guns could be elevated and depressed independently.

HMS *Laforey* was armed with twin 4.7in guns (3x2) in turrets at A, B and X positions, with a single 4in HA/QF mounted in lieu of the after torpedo tubes.

Commenced:	1938
Completed:	1940 (*Larne* and *Laforey* 1941)
Displacement:	1,920 tons (*Laforey* 1,935 tons)
Length:	354ft
Breadth:	37ft
Draught:	10ft
Armament:	*Main* Six 4.7in (3x2 in turrets at A, B, X positions *Lightning, Lookout, Loyal*) Eight 4in (2x4 in shields at A, B, X, Y positions *Lance, Larne, Legion, Lively*) *Secondary* Six smaller *Tubes* Eight 21in (2x4) *AS* Two DC racks on stern, four throwers port and starboard at X, Y positions. 30 DCs carried
Machinery:	Geared turbines on two shafts giving 45,000shp
Max speed:	36.5kts

HISTORICAL NOTES

HMS *Laforey* was torpedoed on 30 March 1944 by U223 off the north coast of Sicily and later sunk.

HMS *Lance* was badly damaged on 22 October 1942 during an air attack on Malta, but was towed to the UK and broken up in 1944.

HMS *Larne* was later renamed *Gurkha* (2) and as this was torpedoed by U133 on 17 January 1942 off Libya.

HMS *Legion* sank on 25 March 1942 after aircraft attack at Malta.

HMS *Lightning* was torpedoed on 12 March 1943 by an Italian MTB off the Libyan Coast.

HMS *Lively* sank after aircraft attack on 11 May 1942 in the eastern Mediterranean.

HMS *Loyal* was mined off the north-east coast of Italy on 12 October 1944, became a constructive total loss and in 1948 was towed to the UK for breaking.

HMS *Lookout*, 'Lightning' class L group, at anchor in 1942. (MoD (Navy))

HMS *Loyal*, 'Lightning' class L group, at anchor with no radar in 1942. (MoD (Navy))

M GROUP

UNIT	BUILDER
Marksman	Scotts SB
(later *Mahratta*)	
Marne	Vickers Armstrong (Tyne)
Martin	Vickers Armstrong (Tyne)
Matchless	Stephen
Meteor	Stephen
Milne (leader)	Scotts SB (completed by John Brown & Co)
Musketeer	Fairfield
Myrmidon	Fairfield

Commenced:	1940 (*Marne* 1939)
Completed:	1941 (*Marne* and *Martin* 1940)
Displacement:	1,920 tons (*Milne* 1,935 tons)
Length:	362ft 6in
Breadth:	37ft
Draught:	10ft
Armament:	*Main* Six 4.7in (3x2 in turrets)
	AA One 4in
	Four 2pdr
	Ten 20mm
	Tubes Four 21in (1x4)
Machinery:	Geared turbines on two shafts giving 48,000shp
Max speed:	36kts

CLASS NOTES

HMS *Marne* and *Matchless* did not carry the 4in gun and did carry eight 21in quadruple tubes (2x4).

This group was the first to mount the main armament in turrets and the guns were power operated.

HISTORICAL NOTES

The Mahratta Brigade of the Indian Army requested that a ship of the Fleet should bear their name, and to comply, and in tribute, the *Marksman* was renamed *Mahratta*.

HMS *Mahratta* (ex-*Marksman*) was torpedoed by U956 on 25 February 1944 when escorting a north Russian convoy.

HMS *Martin* was torpedoed by U431 at the Algerian Landings on 10 November 1942.

HMS *Myrmidon* served with the Polish Navy and was renamed *Orkan*, but was torpedoed on 5 October 1943 in the North Atlantic by U610.

Above: HMS *Marne*, 'Lightning' class M group, leaving harbour in 1942. (MoD (Navy))

Left: HMS *Musketeer*, 'Lightning' class M group, at sea on convoy duty in 1942. (MoD (Navy))

'TOWNS' CLASS

CRAVEN TYPE

UNIT
Lewes (ex-USS *Conway*, ex-USS *Craven*)
St Marys (ex-USS *Bagley*)

BUILDER
Bethlehem SB
Norfolk NY

Commenced:	1918		Secondary Two 3in (23 cal)
Completed:	1919		AA Four MGs
Displacement:	1,020 tons		Tubes 12 21in (4x3)
Length:	342ft	Machinery:	Geared turbines on two shafts giving 25,000shp
Breadth:	35ft		
Draught:	9ft	Max speed:	35kts
Armament:	Main Four 5in (51cal)	Fuel:	400 tons oil

TYPE 4

UNIT	COMMENCED	COMPLETED	BUILDER
Belmont (ex-USS *Saterlee*)	1918	1919	Newport News SB
Beverley (ex-USS *Branch*)	1918	1920	Newport News SB
Bradford (ex-USS *McLanahan*)	1918	1919	Bethlehem SB
Broadwater (ex-USS *Mason*)	1918	1920	Newport News SB
Broadway (ex-USS *Hunt*)	1918	1920	Newport News SB
Burnham (ex-USS *Aulick*)	1918	1919	Bethlehem SB
Burwell (ex-USS *Lamb*)	1918	1919	Bethlehem SB
Buxton (ex-USS *Edwards*)	1918	1919	Bethlehem SB
Cameron (ex-USS *Welles*)	1918	1919	Bethlehem SB
Chesterfield (ex-USS *W.C. Wood*)	1918	1920	Newport News SB
Churchill (ex-USS *Herndon*)	1918	1920	Newport News SB
Clare (ex-USS *A.P. Upshur*)	1918	1920	Newport News SB
Ramsey (ex-USS *Meade*)	1918	1919	Bethlehem SB
Reading (ex-USS *Bailey*)	1919	1919	Bethlehem SB
Ripley (ex-USS *Shubrick*)	1918	1919	Bethlehem SB
Rockingham (ex-USS *Swasey*)	1918	1919	Bethlehem SB
St Croix (ex-USS *McCook*)	1918	1919	Bethlehem SB
St Francis (ex-USS *Bancroft*)	1918	1919	Bethlehem SB
Sherwood (ex-USS *Rodgers*)	1918	1919	Bethlehem SB
Stanley (ex-USS *McCalla*)	1918	1919	Bethlehem SB

HMS *Ramsey*, (ex-American) 'Towns' class, leaving for the Atlantic in 1942. (MoD (Navy))

TYPE 5

UNIT	COMMENCED	COMPLETED	BUILDER
Caldwell (ex-USS *Hale*)	1918	1919	Bath Iron Works
Campbeltown (ex-USS *Buchanan*)	1918	1919	Bath Iron Works
Castleton (ex-USS *Aaron Ward*)	1918	1919	Bath Iron Works
Chelsea (ex-USS *Crowninshield*)	1918	1919	Bath Iron Works
Lancaster (ex-USS *Philip*)	1917	1918	Bath Iron Works
Leamington (ex-USS *Twiggs*)	1918	1919	New York SB
Lincoln (ex-USS *Yarnall*)	1918	1918	Wm Cramp & Sons
Mansfield (ex-USS *Evans*)	1917	1918	Bath Iron Works
Montgomery (ex-USS *Wickes*)	1917	1918	Bath Iron Works
Richmond (ex-USS *Fairfax*)	1917	1918	Mare Is Navy Yd
Salisbury (ex-USS *Claxton*)	1918	1919	Mare Is Navy Yd
Wells (ex-USS *Tillman*)	1918	1921	Charleston N Yd

TYPE 6

UNIT	COMMENCED	COMPLETED	BUILDER
Annapolis (ex-USS *Mackenzie*)	1918	1919	Union Iron Works
Bath (ex-USS *Hopewell*)	1918	1919	Newport News SB
Brighton (ex-USS *Cowell*)	1918	1919	Bethlehem SB
Charlestown (ex-USS *Haraden*)	1918	1919	Newport News SB
Columbia (ex-USS *Haraden*)	1918	1919	Seattle Dry Dock
Georgetown (ex-USS *Maddox*)	1918	1919	Bethlehem SB
Hamilton (ex-USS *Kalk*)	1918	1919	Bethlehem SB
Newark (ex-USS *Ringgold*)	1918	1919	Union Iron Works
Newmarket (ex-USS *Robinson*)	1917	1918	Union Iron Works
Niagara (ex-USS *Thatcher*)	1917	1918	Bethlehem SB
Roxborough (ex-USS *Foote*)	1918	1919	Bethlehem SB
St Albans (ex-USS *Thomas*)	1918	1919	Newport News SB
St Clair (ex-USS *Williams*)	1918	1919	Union Iron Works

TYPE 7

UNIT	COMMENCED	COMPLETED	BUILDER
Leeds (ex-USS *Conner*)	1916	1918	Wm Cramp & Sons
Ludlow (ex-USS *Stockton*)	1916	1918	Wm Cramp & Sons

TYPES 4, 5, 6 and 7

Displacement:	1,190 tons (Type 4) 1,090 tons (Type 5) 1,060 tons (Type 6) 1,020 tons (Type 7)	**Armament:**	*Main* Four 4in (50cal) Five 4in (Type 7; two paired on forecastle) *Secondary* One 3in (23cal) *Tubes* 12 21in (3x4)
Length:	314ft 6in 315ft 6in (Type 7)	**Machinery:**	Geared turbines on two shafts giving 27,000shp (20,000shp Type 7)
Breadth:	30ft 6in	**Max speed:**	35kts 30kts (Type 7)
Draught:	9ft 9in (Type 4) 8ft 9in (Type 5) 8ft 6in (Type 6) 7ft 6in (Type 7)	**Fuel:**	375 tons oil 260 tons oil (Type 7)

CLASS NOTES

These destroyers were transferred to the RN under the terms of the agreement of 2 September 1940, between the governments of the UK and the USA. On transfer, with the exception of HMS *Ludlow* which had three funnels, and HMS *Bradford* which had two funnels, all had four. These destroyers were named after towns and villages with common names in the UK and USA.

HISTORICAL NOTES

The following vessels were transferred to the USSR in 1942: HMS *Chelsea* transferred as *Derzki*, *Roxborough* as *Dublestini*, *St Albans* as *Doistoini*, *Brighton* as *Zharki*, *Leamington* as *Zhguchi*, *Richmond* as *Zhivuchi*, *Georgetown* as *Zhostki*, and *Lincoln* for spares.

HMS *Bath* was torpedoed by U201 whilst escorting a north Russian convoy on 19 August 1941.

HMS *Belmont* was torpedoed by U82 in the North-Western Approaches on 31 December 1941.

HMS *Beverley* was torpedoed by U188 south of Greenland on 10 April 1943 having collided the previous day with the SS *Cairnrona*.

HMS *Leeds*, (ex-American) 'Towns' class; note A gun zareba, 1942. (MoD (Navy))

HMS *Broadwater* was torpedoed by U101 in the western Atlantic on 18 October 1941.

HMS *Cameron* sank after aircraft attack at Portsmouth on 15 December 1940.

HMS *Campbeltown* won immortality by ramming and blowing the outer gates off the Normandie Lock at St Nazaire on 28 March 1942.

Deiatelnyi (ex-HMS *Churchill*) whilst on loan to the USSR was torpedoed in the Arctic on 16 January 1945 by U956.

HMS *Rockingham* on 27 September 1944 was mined and sank off Aberdeen.

HMS *Sherwood* was expended as an air target in May 1943.

HMS *Stanley* was torpedoed by U574 in the Atlantic on 18 December 1941.

HMS *St Croix* (later HMCS) was torpedoed by U305 south of Iceland on 20 September 1943.

HMS *St Francis* (later HMCS) sank after collision with the SS *Winding Gulf* off Sagonnet Point on 14 July 1943.

EX-FRENCH

Unit:	Leopard (ex-*Léopard*)
Commenced:	1922
Completed:	1927
Builders:	Ch de Loire, St Nazaire
Displacement:	2,126 tons
	2,700 tons (full load)
Length:	416ft
Breadth:	37ft 6in

Draught:	17ft 6in
Armament:	*Main* Five 5.1in
	AA Eight 13mm
	Tubes Six 21.7in (2x3)
Machinery:	Turbines on two shafts giving 55,000shp
Max speed:	35.5kts
Range:	900 miles at full speed
Fuel:	550 tons oil

CLASS NOTES

This ship served under the White Ensign in 1940 but was returned to the Free French Navy later on.

A typical French design, with three black cowled raked funnels. She had a greater length than any contemporary RN destroyer at that date.

By the Washington Treaty, this ship would have rated as a cruiser being above 2,000 tons standard displacement tonnage.

HISTORICAL NOTES

HMS *Leopard* served between May and July 1940 with the Portsmouth local flotilla and was manned from HMS *Victory*.

FFS *Léopard* was wrecked near Tobruk on 27 May 1943.

Eight other French destroyers served under the White Ensign from two classes – the 'Pomone' and 'Simoun' classes. All (except *Brandelbras* which was lost) were returned to the French after the war.

HMS *Leopard* (ex-French) at Belfast Lough. (IWM)

'POMONE' CLASS

UNIT	BUILDER
H *Brandelbras*	Normand
H20 *Bouclier*	Ch Worms
H25 *La Cordeliere*	Normand
H63 *La Flore*	At & Ch Bretagne
H47 *L'Incomprise*	Ch Worms
H56 *La Melpomone*	At & Ch Bretagne

Completed:	1935-36
Displacement:	610 tons
Length:	294ft 3in
Breadth:	23ft 9in
Draught:	9ft 3in
Armament:	*Main* Two 3.9in (2x1)
	Secondary Two 37mm (2x1)
	AA Four 13mm (2x2)
	Tubes Two 21.7in (1x2)
Machinery:	Geared turbines on two shafts giving 22,000shp
Max speed:	34kts

HISTORICAL NOTES

Brandelbras used as a harbour training ship at Portsmouth as were all the others except *La Melpomone* which was at the Nore.

Brandelbras foundered in bad weather in the English Channel, 14 December 1940.

'SIMOUN' CLASS

UNIT	BUILDER
HO3 *Mistral*	F & Ch de la Med (Havre)
H16 *Ouragan*	Ch Navales Francais

Completed:	1924-26
Displacement:	1,319 tons
Length:	325ft 3in
Breadth:	33ft 3in
Draught:	13ft 9in
Armament:	*Main* Four 5.1in (4x1)
	AA Two 37mm (2x1)
	Tubes Six 21.7in (2x3)
Machinery:	Geared turbines on two shafts giving 33,000shp
Max speed:	33kts

HISTORICAL NOTES

Mistral was used as tender to HMS *Cardiff* for gunnery training.

Ouragan was used as harbour training ship at Portsmouth.

EX-DUTCH

UNIT	COMPLETED	BUILDER
H35 (ex-G13)	1913	De Schelde
H66 (ex-G15)	1914	Fijenoord

HISTORICAL NOTES

H35 was used as a harbour service craft with the 2nd Submarine Flotilla.

H66 was used as a harbour service craft.

Displacement:	150 tons
Length:	162ft 6in
Breadth:	17ft
Draught:	4ft 6in
Armament:	*Main* Two 3in (2x1)
	Tubes Three 17.7in (3x1)
Machinery:	Reciprocating VTE on one shaft giving 5,500ihp
Max speeds:	25kts

Units:	H97 Blade (ex-Z5), H- (ex-Z6), H93 (ex-Z7), H71 (ex-Z8)
Completed:	1915
Builder:	De Schelde
Displacement:	264 tons
Length:	192ft
Breadth:	19ft 9in
Draught:	5ft 6in

Armament:	*Main* Two 3in (2x1)
	AA Two MGs (2x1)
	Tubes Four 17.7in (1x2, 2x1)
	H97 had no tubes
Machinery:	Reciprocating VTE on two shafts giving 5,500ihp (H97 3,000ihp)
Max speed:	27kts
	22kts (H97)

HMS H35, ex-G13, on a slip. (Koninkrijk der Netherlanden)

Z5 pre-Second World War. (Koninkrijk der Netherlanden)

HMS H66, ex-G15. (Koninkrijk der Netherlanden)

HMS H, ex-Z6. (Koninkrijk der Netherlanden)

HISTORICAL NOTES

RN service covered Plymouth 8th and Harwich 16th Flotillas and the Reserve Fleet, Home Ports.

H97 Blade was used as a tender for the 7th Submarine Flotilla.

H- was used as a harbour service craft at Rosyth and Greenock.

H93 was used as a harbour service craft at Rosyth.

H71 was used as a tender to the 1st and later the 7th Submarine Flotilla.

Royal Netherlands Navy destroyers which sought refuge in UK ports from 1940 for service in the Second World War under the control of the local Royal Naval Flag Officers at the Nore, Portsmouth, Plymouth, Rosyth and other locations as were delegated by the Admiralty and wearing the RN White Ensign or the flag of the Royal Netherlands Navy as was deemed to be most suitable.

Above right: HMS *H93*, ex-Z7. (Koninkrijk der Netherlanden)

Right: HMS *H71*, ex-Z8. (Koninkrijk der Netherlanden)

'HUNT' CLASS

The 'Hunt' class comprised Types 1-4, all designed as convoy escorts, with anti-aircraft capabilities. Nevertheless, they did have an anti-submarine role, destroying five Italian submarines (*Amiraglio Caracciolo, Asteria, Galileo Ferrari, Maggiori Baracca, Narvalo*) and sixteen German ones (U131, U223, U371, U372, U413, U434, U443, U450, U453, U458, U559, U562, U568, U587, U593, U671) – this despite the lack of a 'Hedgehog'. A 2pdr manual bow-chaser was fitted for service on east coast escorts. Of the 'Hunt' class, eighty-six were completed, fourteen transferred to other Allied navies (see below) and seventy-two commissioned by the RN.

Destroyers of the 'Hunt' class transferred to other Allied navies were: *Bolebrook* to Greece as *Pindou*; *Border* to Greece as *Adrias*; *Bedale* to Poland as *Slazak*; *Catterick* to Greece as *Hastings*; *Hatherleigh* to Greece as *Canaris*; *Modbury* to Greece as *Miaoulis*; *Glaisdale* to Norway as *Glaisdale*; *Eskdale* to Norway as *Eskdale*; *Haldon* to France as *La Combattante*; *Oakley* (1) to Poland as *Kujawiak*; *Silverton* to Poland as *Krakowiak*; *Badsworth* to Norway as *Arendalp*; *Bramham* to Greece as *Themistocles*; *Hursley* to Greece as *Kriti*.

HMS *Atherstone*, 'Hunt' class Type 1, at launch. (Cammell Laird SB)

TYPE 1

UNIT	COMPLETED	BUILDER
Atherstone	1940	Cammell Laird
Berkeley	1940	Cammell Laird
Cattistock	1940	Yarrow
Cleveland	1941	Yarrow
Cotswold	1941	Yarrow
Cottesmore	1940	Yarrow
Eglinton	1940	Vickers-Armstrong (Tyne)
Exmoor	1940	Vickers-Armstrong (Tyne)
Fernie	1941	John Brown
Garth	1940	John Brown
Hambledon	1940	Swan Hunter
Holderness	1940	Swan Hunter
Mendip	1940	Swan Hunter
Meynell	1940	Swan Hunter
Pytchley	1940	Scotts SB
Quantock	1940	Scotts SB
Quorn	1940	White
Southdown	1940	White
Tynedale	1940	Stephen
Whaddon	1941	Stephen

Commenced:	1939
Displacement:	1,000 tons
Length:	280ft
Breadth:	29ft
Draught:	7ft 9in
Armament:	*Main* Four 4in
	Secondary Four 2pdr
	AA Two 20mm
	AS 70 DCs carried
Machinery:	Geared turbines on two shafts giving 19,000shp
Max speed:	30kts
Range:	2,000 miles at 12kts
Fuel:	280 tons oil

CLASS NOTES

This class of destroyer was designed as a convoy escort but was unable to cross the Atlantic without RAS which was in its infancy in the early years of the Second World War. The 'Hunt' class saw the end, for the time being, of the trend towards large tonnage destroyers.

HISTORICAL NOTES

HMS *Berkeley* was severely damaged off Dieppe by aircraft attack, and had to be sunk by her own forces on 19 August 1942 by gunfire of HMS *Albrighton*.

HMS *Exmoor* was torpedoed by an E-boat off Lowestoft and sank on 25 February 1941.

HMS *Quorn* sank after the warhead from a German human torpedo was attached and detonated, whilst she was on patrol off the Normandy Beachhead on 2 August 1944.

HMS *Tynedale* was torpedoed by U593 on 12 December 1943 in the western Mediterranean.

HMS *Eglington*, 'Hunt' class Type 1, at sea; note bowchaser. (MoD (Navy))

TYPE 2

UNIT	COMMENCED	COMPLETED	BUILDER
Avonvale	1940	1941	John Brown
Badsworth	1940	1941	Cammell Laird
Beaufort	1939	1941	Cammell Laird

Bedale	1940	1942	Hawthorn Leslie
Bicester	1940	1941	Hawthorn Leslie
Blackmore	1941	1942	Stephen
Blankney	1941	1942	John Brown
Blencathra	1939	1940	Cammell Laird
Bramham	1941	1942	Stephen
Brocklesby	1939	1941	Cammell Laird
Calpe	1941	1942	Swan Hunter
Chiddingfold	1940	1941	Scotts SB
Cowdray	1940	1942	Scotts SB
Croome	1940	1941	Stephen
Dulverton	1940	1941	Stephen
Eridge	1939	1940	Swan Hunter
Exmoor (ex-*Burton*)	1940	1941	Swan Hunter
Farndale	1939	1941	Swan Hunter
Grove	1939	1941	Swan Hunter
Heythrop	1939	1941	Swan Hunter
Hursley	1940	1941	Swan Hunter
Hurworth	1939	1941	Vickers Armstrong (Tyne)
Lamerton	1939	1940	Swan Hunter
Lauderdale	1940	1941	Thornycroft
Ledbury	1940	1942	Thornycroft
Liddesdale	1939	1940	Vickers Armstrong (Tyne)
Middleton	1940	1941	Vickers Armstrong (Tyne)
Oakley	1940	1941	Vickers Armstrong (Tyne)
Puckeridge	1940	1941	White
Silverton	1939	1941	White
Southwold	1940	1942	White
Tetcott	1940	1941	White
Tickham	1941	1942	Yarrow
Wheatland	1940	1941	Yarrow
Wilton	1941	1942	Yarrow
Zetland	1941	1942	Yarrow

HMS *Badsworth*, 'Hunt' class Type 2, leaving the fitting-out basin under tow on the River Mersey. (Cammell Laird SB)

Displacement:	1,025 tons
	1,490 tons (full load)
Length:	280ft
Breadth:	31ft 6in
Draught:	7ft 6in
Armament:	*Main* Six 4in (3x2)
	AA Two 40mm (2x1), four 2pdr (1x4)
	AS Four DC throwers, 60 DCs carried
Machinery:	Geared turbines on shafts giving
	19,000shp
Max speed:	29kts
Range:	3,600nm radius at 14kts
Fuel:	275 tons oil

CLASS NOTES

This was the second class of utility escort destroyer for rapid construction. The Type 2s escorted Atlantic convoys.

HISTORICAL NOTES

HMS *Dulverton* sank after being hit by a glider bomb off Kos on 13 November 1943.

HMS *Grove* sank on 15 June 1942 after aircraft attack in the central Mediterranean.

HMS *Heythrop* was torpedoed by U652 off the Libyan coast on 20 March 1942.

HMS *Hurworth* was mined and sank in the Aegean on 22 October 1943.

HMS *Oakley* (1) became HMS *Kujawiak* (Polish) and as such was sunk off Malta on 15 June 1942 after being mined.

HMS *Puckeridge* was torpedoed by U617 in the Mediterranean off Gibraltar on 6 September 1943.

HMS *Southwold* was mined on 24 March 1942 and sank off Malta.

HMS *Tickham* later became HMS *Oakley* (2).

HMS *Bedale*, 'Hunt' class Type 2, entering harbour in 1943. (MoD (Navy))

HMS *Zetland*, 'Hunt' class Type 2, in 1943; note AA radar. (MoD (Navy))

TYPE 3

UNIT	COMMENCED	COMPLETED	BUILDER
Airedale	1941	1942	John Brown
Albrighton	1940	1941	John Brown
Aldenham	1941	1942	Cammell Laird
Belvoir	1940	1942	Cammell Laird
Blean	1941	1942	Hawthorn Leslie
Bleasdale	1940	1941	Vickers Armstrong (Tyne)
Bolebrook	1940	1941	Swan Hunter
Border	1941	1942	Swan Hunter
Catterick	1940	1941	Vickers Armstrong (Barrow)
Derwent	1940	1941	Vickers Armstrong (Barrow)
Easton	1941	1942	White
Eggesford	1941	1942	White
Eskdale	1941	1942	Cammell Laird
Glaisdale	1941	1942	Cammell Laird
Goathland	1942	1943	Fairfield
La Combattante (ex-Haldon)	1941	1942	Fairfield
Hatherleigh	1940	1941	Vickers Armstrong (Tyne)
Haydon	1941	1942	Vickers Armstrong (Tyne)
Holcombe	1941	1942	Stephen
Limbourne	1941	1942	Stephen
Melbreak	1941	1942	Swan Hunter
Modbury	1941	1942	Swan Hunter
Penylan	1941	1942	Vickers Armstrong (Barrow)
Rockwood	1941	1942	Vickers Armstrong (Barrow)
Stevenstone	1941	1943	White
Talybont	1941	1943	White
Tanatside	1941	1942	Yarrow
Wensleydale	1941	1942	Yarrow

Displacement: 1,037 tons
Length: 280ft
Breadth: 31ft 3in
Draught: 7ft 3in
Armament: Main Four 4in (2x2)
AA Four 2pdr, Two 20mm (or 40mm)
Tubes Two 21in
AS Four DC throwers
60 DCs carried
Machinery: Geared turbines on twin shafts giving 19,000shp
Max speed: 28kts
Range: 3,700 miles radius at 14kts
Fuel: 275 tons oil

HISTORICAL NOTES

HMS *Airedale* was bombed off Sollum on 16 June 1942.

HMS *Aldenham* was mined on 14 December and sank in the Adriatic.

HMS *Blean* was torpedoed by U443 off Oran on 11 December 1942.

HMS *Eskdale*, whilst in Norwegian service, was torpedoed on 14 April 1943 by an E-boat off the Lizard, in the English Channel.

HMS *Haldon* (*La Combattante*) was mined in the North Sea on 23 February 1945.

HMS *Holcombe* was torpedoed by U593 off Bougie on 12 December 1943.

HMS *Limbourne* was torpedoed on 23 October 1943 by an E-boat in the English Channel and later sunk by own forces.

HMS *Penylan* was torpedoed by an E-boat in the English Channel on 2 December 1942.

HMS *Aldenham*, 'Hunt' class Type 3, leaving the fitting-out basin on the River Mersey. (Cammell Laird SB)

HMS *Catterick*, 'Hunt' class Type 3, leaving harbour passing Walney Island. Aft of the funnel may be seen the multiple Pom-Poms on its own deckhouse. (Vickers)

HMS *Derwent*, 'Hunt' class Type 3, leaving harbour passing Walney Island. The RDF antenna is positioned below and forward of the bridge, the supporting structure being between the magazine ventilator cowls. (Vickers)

TYPE 4

Units:	*Brecon, Brissenden*		*AA* Four 2pdr
Commenced:	1941		Two 40mm
Completed:	1942		Two 20mm
Builder:	Thornycroft		*Tubes* Three 21in (1x3)
Displacement:	1,175 tons		*AS* Four DC throwers
Length:	296ft	**Machinery:**	Geared turbines on two shafts giving
Breadth:	33ft 6in		19,000shp
Draught:	9ft	**Max speed:**	25kts
Armament:	*Main* Six 4in (3x2)	**Range:**	3,500 miles at 14kts

CLASS NOTES

These two ships were designed as anti-aircraft vessels for service in northern latitudes and as escort vessels, having double decks fore and aft.

Below: HMS *Brecon*, 'Hunt' class Type 4, at sea in 1943. (MoD (Navy))

Bottom: HMS *Brissenden*, 'Hunt' class Type 4, at sea in 1949. (MoD (Navy))

EX-BRAZILIAN 'H' CLASS

UNIT	BUILDER
Harvester (ex-*Handy*, ex-*Jurua*)	Vickers Armstrong (Barrow)
Havant (ex-*Javary*)	White
Havelock (ex-*Jutahy*)	White
Hesperus (ex-*Hearty*, ex-*Juruena*)	Thornycroft
Highlander (ex-*Jaguaribe*)	Thornycroft
Hurricane (ex-*Japarua*)	Vickers Armstrong (Barrow)

Commenced:	1939
Completed:	1940
Displacement:	1,400 tons
Length:	323ft
Breadth:	33ft
Draught:	8ft 6in
Armament:	*Main* Three 4.7in
	AA Seven smaller
	Tubes Eight 21in (2x4)
Machinery:	Geared turbines on two shafts giving 34,000shp
Max speed:	35.5kts
Fuel:	450 tons oil

CLASS NOTES

These six destroyers arrived at a very important stage of the war, being quickly completed to act as escorts and AS vessels. All were based on the 'H' class design but upon completion lacked Y gun, a possible reason being that they were intended for use as minelayers.

HISTORICAL NOTES

The body of Capt F.J. Walker CB, DSO and three bars, RN, who died on 8 July 1944, was committed to the deep from HMS *Hesperus* off Liverpool Bar Light Ship. Capt Walker had been in command of Second Escort Group.

HMS *Harvester* was torpedoed on 11 March 1943 by U432 in the western Atlantic.

HMS *Hurricane* was torpedoed on 24 December 1943 by U275 north-east of the Azores.

HMS *Havant* was attacked on 1 June 1940 by enemy aircraft off Dunkirk.

Early in May 1941, HMS *Hurricane* whilst at Liverpool was bombed and sunk but salvage being possible, she was raised, then refitted and was back with the fleet by January 1942.

HMS *Havant*, (ex-Brazilian) 'H' class, at sea in 1940. (MoD (Navy))

HMS *Harvester* leaving Barrow-in-Furness via Walney Channel. (Vickers)

EX-TURKISH

Units:	*Ithuriel (ex-Gayret), Inconstant (ex-Muavenet)*	**Armament:**	*Main* Four 4.7in (4x1 in shields)
Commenced:	1939		*AA* Six 40mm
Completed:	1942		*Tubes* Eight 21in (2x4)
Builders:	Vickers Armstrong (Barrow)		*AS* Four DC throwers
Displacement:	1,360 tons	**Machinery:**	Geared turbine on two shafts giving
	2,100 tons (full load)		34,000shp
Length:	323ft	**Max speed:**	35.5kts
Breadth:	33ft	**Range:**	5,000 miles at 15kts
Draught:	8ft 6in	**Fuel:**	450 tons oil

HMS *Ithuriel* (ex-Turkish) off Walney Island on builder's trials, lacking radar, 1940. (Vickers)

HMS *Inconstant* (ex-Turkish) entering Barrow on builder's trials. (Vickers)

CLASS NOTES

These two ships were very similar in appearance and other details to the 'Intrepid' class of the RN.

Two other ships of this class, HMS *Demir Hisar* and *Sultan Hisar*, were under construction by Denny and sailed with RN crews under the White Ensign, acting as anti-submarine escorts for their delivery voyage to Turkey. Details of the use of these vessels are given below by courtesy of the Naval Historical Branch, Ministry of Defence.

HISTORICAL NOTES

HMS *Ithuriel* was badly damaged by boming in Bone Harbour 1942. It was decided not to repair her, but later she was reduced to care and maintenance and in February 1943 she was used as a base for training Italian anti-submarine personnel. She was later towed to the UK and broken up at Inverkeithing in 1945. In her short eight months of active service HMS *Ithuriel* served in force H, took part in Operation Pedestal, and sank the Italian submarine *Cobalto* on 12 August 1942.

After being damaged, HMS *Oribi* replaced her and took the name *Ithuriel*.

Demir Hisar and *Sultan Hisar* were manned by British crews drawn from Portsmouth and Devonport respectively. They carried a full engine-room complement but only half the normal upper-deck complement, the remaining accommodation being used for suitable ratings awaiting passage. They sailed to Turkey via the Cape in two separate convoys in which they were employed as AS escorts and both journeys appear to have been without incident.

HMS *Sultan Hisar* sailed from the Clyde on 22 December 1941 in company with HMS *Wivern*, *Active* and the armed merchant cruisers *Alaunia*, *Chitral*, *Worcestershire* and *Pretoria Castle* which were carrying service personnel. She arrived at Alexandria on 7 February 1942 where boiler cleaning, painting and minor repairs were carried out before finally sailing for Turkey on 17 February. On 19 February the *Sultan Hisar* arrived at Alexandretta where a ceremonial change of flags took place. The C-in-C Mediterranean reported that the Turkish authorities were very cordial and grateful for the safe arrival of the ship.

HMS *Demir Hisar* sailed from the Clyde on 11 January 1942 as one of the AS escorts in convoy WS15. She arrived in Cape Town on 9 February with Vice-Admiral 3rd Battle Squadron (Vice-Adm W.E.C. Tait CB, MVO) temporarily embarked from HMS *Resolution*, and reached Alexandria on 14 March. She sailed again on 28 March, and the C-in-C Mediterranean reported on 4 April that the *Demir Hisar* had been handed over to Turkey.

'O' ('OBDURATE') CLASS

UNIT	BUILDER
Obdurate	Denny
Obedient	Denny
Offa	Fairfield
Onslaught (ex-*Pathfinder*)	Fairfield
Onslow (ex-*Pakenham*)	John Brown
Opportune	Thornycroft
Oribi (ex-*Observer*)	Fairfield
Orwell	Thornycroft

Commenced:	1940 (*Opportune* and *Onslaught* 1941)
Completed:	1942 (*Oribi* and *Offa* 1941)
Displacement:	1,540 tons (*Onslow* 1,550 tons)
	2,625 tons (full load)
Length:	345ft
Breadth:	35ft
Draught:	9ft
Armament:	*Main* Four 4.7in
	(Minelayers had three 4in at A, B, X
	positions)
	AA Four 2pdr
	Three 40mm
	Tubes Eight 21in (2x4)
	AS Four DC throwers, 70DCs carried
Machinery:	Geared turbines on two shafts giving
	40,000shp
Max speed:	34kts

CLASS NOTES

This class were given old type 4in guns in 'lengthened shields'. They also had the distinction of being the first destroyers of the War Construction Programme. *Obdurate*, *Opportune*, *Orwell* and *Obedient* were all fitted out for minelaying.

The 'O' to 'Z' classes were designed on the hull of the 'Javelin' class and although the dimensions vary, the 'Javelins' were very 'wet' and consequently the 'O' to 'Z' classes were given more sheer from the bow to the break of the forecastle.

HISTORICAL NOTES

No war losses.

HMS *Offa*, 'O' class, at anchor in 1945. (MoD (Navy))

'P' ('PALADIN') CLASS

UNIT	COMMENCED	COMPLETED	BUILDER
Pakenham (ex-*Onslow*)	1941	1942	Hawthorn Leslie
Paladin	1940	1941	John Brown
Panther	1941	1942	Vickers Armstrong (Barrow)
Partridge	1941	1942	Fairfield
Pathfinder (ex-*Onslaught*)	1940	1941	Hawthorn Leslie
Penn	1940	1941	Vickers Armstrong (Tyne)
Petard (ex-*Persistent*)	1939	1942	Vickers Armstrong (Tyne)
Porcupine	1940	1941	Vickers Armstrong (Tyne)

Displacement:	1,825 tons
	2,400 tons (full load)
Length:	354ft
Breadth:	35ft
Draught:	15ft 9in
Armament:	*Main* Four 4in
	AA Four 40mm
	Two 20mm
	Tubes Eight 21in (2x4)
Machinery:	Geared turbines on two shafts giving
	40,000shp
Max speed:	34kts

HMS *Pathfinder*, 'P' class, at anchor off Plymouth breakwater. (MoD (Navy))

CLASS NOTES

These were very similar vessels to the 'O' class, having virtually the same dimensions. Y gun was mounted without a shield.

HISTORICAL NOTES

HMS *Pakenham* (ex-*Onslow*) sank on 17 April 1943 after hits from Italian shore batteries on the coast of western Sicily.

HMS *Paladin* and *Petard* attacked and sank the Japanese submarine 127 60 miles from Addu Atoll on 12 February 1944.

HMS *Panther* sank after aircraft attack on 9 October 1943 in the Scarpanto Channel.

HMS *Partridge* was torpedoed on 18 December 1942 by U565 west of Oran.

'Q' ('QUEENBOROUGH') CLASS

UNIT	BUILDER
Quadrant	Hawthorn Leslie
Quail	Hawthorn Leslie
Quality	Swan Hunter
Queenborough	Swan Hunter
Quiberon	White
Quickmatch	White
Quilliam (leader)	Hawthorn Leslie
Quentin	White

Commenced:	1940 (*Quickmatch* and *Quail* 1941)
Completed:	1942 (*Quilliam* 1941)
Displacement:	1,650 tons
	2,150 tons (full load)
Length:	358ft
Breadth:	36ft
Draught:	16ft max
Armament:	*Main* Four 4.7in
	One 4in (aft of funnel)
	AA four 40mm
	Six 20mm
	Tubes Eight 21in (2x4)
	AS Four DC throwers
Machinery:	Geared turbines on two shafts giving
	40,000shp
Max speed:	34kts

CLASS NOTES

This class had a much improved overall armament and were slightly larger vessels than the 'O' and 'P' classes.

HISTORICAL NOTES

HMS *Quail* was mined on 15 November 1945 and sank in the Adriatic.

HMS *Quentin* on 2 December 1942 sank after being struck by an aircraft-launched torpedo off Galita Island.

HMS *Quiberon* and *Quickmatch* were transferred to the Royal Australian Navy in 1943, and *Queenborough*, *Quality* and *Quadrant* followed in 1945.

HMS *Quilliam* was transferred to the Royal Netherlands Navy in 1945.

HMS *Quickmatch*, 'Q' class, entering harbour in 1942. (MoD (Navy))

HMS *Quality*, 'Q' class, at anchor in 1942. (MoD (Navy))

'R' ('ROTHERHAM') CLASS

UNIT	BUILDER
Racehorse	John Brown
Raider	Cammell Laird
Rapid	Cammell Laird
Redoubt	John Brown
Relentless	John Brown
Rocket	Scotts SB
Roebuck	Scotts SB (Completed by John Brown)
Rotherham (leader)	John Brown

CLASS NOTES

This class represents the typical Royal Navy destroyer type of the Second World War. It was the first to have officers' quarters forward instead of aft.

HISTORICAL NOTES

No war losses.

Commenced:	1941
Completed:	1942 (*Rapid, Rocket, Roebuck*, 1943)
Displacement:	1,735 tons (*Rotherham* 1,750 tons)
	2,495 tons (full load; *Rotherham*
	2,510 tons)
Length:	358ft
Breadth:	36ft
Draught:	9ft 6in
Armament:	*Main* Four 4.7in
	One 4in (aft of funnel)
	AA Four 2pdr, four 40mm, six 20mm
	Tubes Eight 21in (2x4)
	AS Four DC throwers
Machinery:	Geared turbines on two shafts giving
	40,000shp
Max speed:	34kts
Fuel:	490 tons oil

Top: HMS *Raider*, 'R' class, leaving the fitting-out basin on the River Mersey in minimum visibility conditions. The main longwire aerials are stretched from the fore to a dwarf mast at the rear of the searchlight platform, even though there is a main lattice mast. (Cammell Laird SB)

Centre: HMS *Racehorse*, 'R' class, entering harbour in 1942. (MoD (Navy))

Above: HMS *Rapid*, 'R' class, leaving the Mersey after commissioning, 1943. Clearly visible are the gunnery radar positioned above the director, sea boat and motorboat on the starboard main deck abreast the funnel, multiple Pom-Poms abreast the motorboat midships, the two quadruple torpedo mountings with the searchlight platform in between, a single 20mm lower than the searchlight on both beams, twin depth charge throwers abreast of X gun and depth charge racks on the stern. (Cammell Laird SB)

'S' ('SAVAGE') CLASS

UNIT	BUILDER
Saumarez (leader)	Hawthorn Leslie
Savage	Hawthorn Leslie
Scorpion (ex-*Sentinel*)	Cammell Laird
Scourge	Cammell Laird
Serapis	Scotts SB
Shark	Scotts SB
Success (later *Stord*)	White
Swift	White

Commenced:	1941 (*Success* 1942)
Completed:	1943
Displacement:	1,730 tons
	2,535 tons (full load)
Length:	363ft
Breadth:	36ft
Draught:	10ft 6in
Armament:	*Main* Four 4.7in (4x1)
	(*Savage* Four 4.5in (1x2, 2x1))
	AA Four 40mm
	Tubes Eight 21in (2x4)
Machinery:	Geared turbines on two shafts developing 40,000shp
Max speed:	36kts
Range:	2,600 miles at 22kts
Fuel:	580 tons oil

CLASS NOTES

This and classes to similar designs were constructed with war worthiness first and outward appearances second, yet despite this condition they were a very handsome type and their performance was second to none. They had a redesigned gunshield.

HISTORICAL NOTES

HMS *Saumarez* was lost in 1946 in the Corfu Channel when she struck an Albanian mine which had been laid in an International waterway. (See HMS *Volage*.)

On the fore deck of HMS *Savage* was mounted the prototype 4.5in twin turret of the 'Battle' class design.

HMS *Shark* whilst named *Svenner* and on loan to the Royal Norwegian Navy was torpedoed by German E-boats on 6 June 1944 off the Normandy beachhead.

HMS *Swift* was mined and sank off the Normandy beachhead on 24 June 1944.

HMS *Scourge*, 'S' class, leaving the fitting-out basin on the River Mersey. (Cammell Laird SB)

HMS *Savage*, 'S' class, 1942 with a twin 4.5in turret in A position on the forecastle (prototype for the later 'Battle' classes) and 4.5in guns in single mounting at X and Y positions. (Swan Hunter)

HMS *Scorpion*, 'S' class, leaving the fitting-out basin on the River Mersey. (Cammell Laird SB)

'T' ('TROUBRIDGE') CLASS

UNIT	BUILDER
Teazer	Cammell Laird
Tenacious	Cammell Laird
Termagant	Denny
Terpsichore	Denny
Troubridge (leader)	John Brown
Tumult	John Brown
Tuscan	Swan Hunter
Tyrian	Swan Hunter

CLASS NOTES

Another of the very similar destroyer classes under construction at this period. These ships were largely of all-welded build.

HMS *Tumult* was completed with two additional fixed tubes experimentally which were later removed.

HISTORICAL NOTES

No war losses.

Commenced:	1941
Completed:	1943
Displacement:	1,927 tons
	2,745 tons (full load)
Length:	363ft
Breadth:	36ft
Draught:	10ft
Armament:	*Main* Four 4.7in
	AA Four 2pdr, four 20mm
	Tubes Eight 21in (2x4)
Machinery:	Geared turbines on two shafts giving
	40,000shp
Max speed:	36kts

Below: HMS *Teazer*, 'T' class, leaving the fitting-out basin on the River Mersey under tow for builder's trials in 1943. (Cammell Laird SB)

Bottom: HMS *Tenacious*, 'T' class, steaming down Formby Channel, River Mersey, on builder's trials. (Cammell Laird SB)

'U' ('ULSTER') CLASS

UNIT	COMMENCED	COMPLETED	BUILDER
Grenville (leader)	1941	1943	Swan Hunter
Ulster	1941	1943	Swan Hunter
Ulysses	1942	1943	Cammell Laird
Undaunted	1942	1944	Cammell Laird
Undine	1943	1943	Thornycroft
Urania	1942	1944	Vickers Armstrong (Barrow)
Urchin	1942	1943	Vickers Armstrong (Barrow)
Ursa	1942	1944	Thornycroft

Displacement:	1,710 tons
	2,530 tons (full load)
Length:	362ft 9in
Breadth:	35ft 9.6in
Draught:	10ft
Armament:	*Main* Four 4.7in
	AA Four 40mm
	Four 20mm
	Tubes Eight 21in (2x4)
Machinery:	Geared turbines on two shafts giving 40,000shp
Max speed:	36.75kts

CLASS NOTES

A further class of fleet destroyers built to similar design as the preceding class. They were well built and lasting, with good sea-keeping qualities. Although the tubes were quadruple, the mountings were quintuple with the centre tube removed.

HISTORICAL NOTES

No war losses.

HMS *Undaunted*, 'U' class, on the Mersey for builder's trials with the searchlight platform aft of the funnel, main armament trained to port. (Cammell Laird SB)

HMS *Urchin*, 'U' class, passing Walney Island on builder's trials. (Vickers)

HMS *Grenville* as converted from a destroyer to a Type 15 frigate post-Second World War. (Fleet Photographic Unit, Portsmouth)

HMS *Undaunted* as converted from a destroyer to a frigate post-Second World War. (Fleet Photographic Unit, Portsmouth)

'V' ('VIGILANT') CLASS

UNIT	BUILDER
Hardy (leader)	John Brown
Valentine (ex-*Kempenfelt*, later HMCS *Algonquin*)	John Brown
Venus	Fairfield
Verulam	Fairfield
Vigilant	Swan Hunter
Virago	Swan Hunter
Vixen (later HMCS *Sioux*)	White
Volage	White

Commenced:	1942 (*Hardy* 1941)
Completed:	1943 (*Volage, Valentine, Vixen* 1944)
Displacement:	1,730 tons
	2,530 tons (full load)
Length:	363ft
Breadth:	36ft
Draught:	13ft
Armament:	*Main* Three/Four 4.7in
	AA Six 40mm, Two 20mm
	Tubes Eight 21in (2x4)
Machinery:	Geared turbines on two shafts giving 40,000shp
Max speed:	36.75kts

CLASS NOTES

This was another of the standard utility classes which were built in flotillas of eight. It should be noted that prior to 1939 the practice in planning flotillas was to have eight destroyers and one leader. Later it was decided that a flotilla would consist of eight destroyers but one of the eight would be the leader, being indistinguishable from the other ships of the class. The practice was maintained, however, of naming the leader after a notable captain or admiral.

HISTORICAL NOTES

HMS *Hardy* whilst leader of a JW convoy close escort was torpedoed with an acoustic torpedo by U278 off Bear Island on 30 January 1944, and had to be sunk by own forces.

HMS *Volage* had her bow blown off in 1946 after she was mined in the Corfu Channel which is an international waterway bounding Albania (see HMS *Saumarez*), but was later towed to and repaired at Malta Dockyard.

HMS *Verulam*, 'V' class, at anchor in 1943. (MoD (Navy))

HMS *Venus*, 'V' class, at anchor in 1944. (MoD (Navy))

'W' ('WAKEFUL') CLASS

UNIT	BUILDER
Kempenfelt (leader) (ex-Valentine)	John Brown
Wager	John Brown
Wakeful (ex-Zebra)	Fairfield
Wessex (ex-Zenith)	Fairfield
Whelp	Hawthorn Leslie
Whirlwind	Hawthorn Leslie
Wizard	Vickers Armstrong (Barrow)
Wrangler	Vickers Armstrong (Barrow)

Commenced:	1942
Completed:	1944 (*Kempenfelt* 1,730 tons)
	2,505 tons (full load)
	(*Kempenfelt* 2,525 tons full load)
Length:	363ft
Breadth:	36ft
Draught:	16ft max
Armament:	*Main* Four 4.7in
	AA Five 40mm, Two 20mm
	Tubes Eight 21in (2x4)
	AS Four DC throwers
Machinery:	Geared turbines on two shafts giving 40,000shp
Max speed:	36.75kts

HMS *Wizard*, 'W' class, leaving harbour in Walney Channel for trials. (Vickers)

CLASS NOTES

Similar in most respects to the preceding 'V' class. This class had a heavier main and anti-submarine armament, also a smaller main director than ships of the 'W' class.

HISTORICAL NOTES

No war losses.

HMS *Wrangler*, 'W' class, leaving harbour after commissioning, passing Walney Island. (Vickers)

'Z' ('ZAMBESI') CLASS

UNIT	BUILDER	UNIT	BUILDER
Myngs (leader)	Vickers Armstrong (Tyne)	*Zenith* (ex-*Wessex*)	Denny
Zambesi	Cammell Laird	*Zephyr*	Vickers Armstrong (Tyne)
Zealous	Cammell Laird	*Zest*	Thornycroft
Zebra (ex-*Wakeful*)	Denny	*Zodiac*	Thornycroft

Commenced:	1942
Completed:	1944
Displacement:	1,710 tons (*Myngs* 1,730 tons)
	2,555 tons (full load; *Myngs* 2,575 tons)
Length:	363ft
Breadth:	36ft
Draught:	16ft max
Armament:	*Main* Three/Four 4.5in
	AA Six 40mm (*Myngs* Two 2pdr, three 40mm)
	Tubes Eight 21in (2x4) (*Myngs* Four 21in (1x4))
	AS Four DC throwers
Machinery:	Geared turbines on two shafts giving 40,000shp
Max speed:	34kts

CLASS NOTES

This was the first class of 4.5in-gunned destroyers, also they had a larger forward director then the 'W' class. *Zambesi* had only four tubes, and she and *Zephyr* had no Y gun, being intended for mine laying.

The 4.5in gun mounted from this class onwards including the prototype mounted on HMS *Savage*, used a 5lb heavier shell with a muzzle velocity of 200ft/sec less.

All ships from the 'O' to 'Z' classes had at least four depth charge throwers.

HISTORICAL NOTES
No war losses.

HMS *Zest*, 'Z' class, at anchor in 1944. (MoD (Navy))

HMS *Zambesi*, 'Z' class, under tow leaving the fitting-out basin on the River Mersey. (Cammell Laird SB)

'C' CLASS

The 'C' class as built formed four flotillas grouped into four sub-classes with 'Ca', 'Ch', 'Co' and 'Cr' names. All were built to War Emergency designs and all-welded construction.

CAESAR/'Ca' GROUP

UNIT	BUILDER	UNIT	BUILDER
Caesar (ex-*Ranger*) (leader)	John Brown	*Carysfort*	White
Cambrian (ex-*Spitfire*)	Scotts SB (fitted out by John Brown)	*Cassandra* (ex-*Tourmaline*)	Yarrow
		Cavalier	White
Caprice (ex- *Swallow*)	Yarrow	*Cavendish* (ex-*Sibyl*)	John Brown
Carron (ex-*Strenuous*)	Scotts SB		

Commenced:	1943 (*Cambrian, Caprice, Carron* 1942)
Completed:	1944
Displacement:	1,710 tons
	2,560 tons (full load)
Length:	362ft 9in
Breadth:	38ft
Draught:	10ft
Armament:	*Main* Four 4.5in
	AA Six 40mm
	Two/Six 20mm or 2pdr
	Tubes Eight 21in (2x4)
	AS Four DC throwers (replaced by two Squid)
Machinery:	Geared turbines on two shafts giving 40,000shp
Max speed:	36.7kts

CLASS NOTES

Some ships were armed with a Squid in X position, this necessitated the X 4.5in gun to be suppressed and twin 40mm fitted forward of the Squid. See photograph of HMS *Carysfort*.

HISTORICAL NOTES

No war losses.

HMS *Carron*, 'C' class Ca group, leaving harbour in 1945. (MoD (Navy))

:HMS *Carysfort*, 'C' class Ca group, entering the harbour, 1957. Note twin Squid in place of X gun. (MoD (Navy))

CHAPLET/'Ch' GROUP

UNIT	BUILDER
Chaplet	Thornycroft
Charity	Thornycroft
Chequers (leader)	Scotts SB
Cheviot	Stephen
Chevron	Stephen
Chieftain (leader)	Scotts SB
Childers (ex-*Pellew*)	Denny
Chivalrous	Denny

Commenced:	1943
Completed:	1945 (*Chieftain* and *Chivalrous* 1946)
Displacement:	1,710 tons
	2,560 tons (full load)
Length:	362ft 9in
Breadth:	36ft
Draught:	10ft
Armament:	*Main* Four 4.5in
	AA Six 40mm
	Two/Six 20 mm or 2pdr
	Tubes Eight 21in (2x4)
	AS Four DC throwers (replaced by two Squid)
Machinery:	Geared turbines on two shafts giving 40,000shp
Max speed:	36.75kts

CLASS NOTES

All to the same design as the 'Ca' group, HMS *Chaplet* and *Chieftain* were fitted out as minelayers, but with one 4.5in gun less.

HISTORICAL NOTES

HMS *Charity* served in support of British and United Nations forces from the start of the Korean War.

HMS *Chaplet*, 'C' class Ch group, at sea in 1945. (MoD (Navy))

HMS *Chieftain*, 'C' class Ch group, at sea in 1946. (MoD (Navy))

COCKADE/'Co' GROUP

UNIT	COMPLETED	BUILDER
Cockade	1945	Yarrow
Comet	1945	Yarrow
Comus	1946	Thornycroft
Concord (ex-*Corso*)	1946	Thornycroft
Consort	1946	Stephen
Constance (leader)	1944	Vickers Armstrong (Tyne)
Contest	1945	White
Cossack (leader)	1945	Vickers Armstrong (Tyne)

Commenced:	1943
Displacement:	1,710 tons
	2,560 tons (full load)
Length:	362ft 9in
Breadth:	36ft
Draught:	10ft
Armament:	*Main* Four 4.5in
	AA Six 40mm, Two/Six 20mm or 2pdr
	Tubes Four DC throwers (replaced by two Squid)
Machinery:	Geared turbines on two shafts giving 40,000shp
Max speed:	36.75kts

CLASS NOTES

All designed and built to the same specifications as the 'Ch' group. HMS *Comet* and *Contest* were minelayers and lacked the sternmost 4.5in gun. (See photograph of HMS *Contest*.)

HISTORICAL NOTES

HMS *Concord* and *Consort* took part in the 'Yangtse Incident' in 1949. Later HMS *Cockade, Comus, Concord, Consort, Constance* and *Cossack* were a part of the Royal Naval supporting forces to the United Nations armies in Korea.

HMS *Contest*, 'C' class Co group, in 1957. Note minelaying rails with X and Y guns suppressed. (MoD (Navy))

HMS *Concord*, 'C' class Co group, at sea in 1946. Note walkways above tubes. (MoD (Navy))

CRESCENT/'Cr' GROUP

UNIT	COMMENCED	COMPLETED	BUILDER
Creole	1944	1946	White
Crescent (leader)	1943	1945	John Brown
Crispin (ex-*Craccher*)	1944	1946	White
Cromwell (ex-*Cretan*)	1943	1945	Scotts SB
Crown	1944	1947	Scotts SB
Croziers	1944	1945	Yarrow
Crusader (leader)	1943	1945	John Brown
Crystal	1944	1946	Yarrow

Displacement:	1,710 tons
	2,560 tons (full load)
Length:	362ft 9in
Breadth:	36ft
Draught:	10ft
Armament:	*Main* Four 4.5in
	AA Six 40mm, Two/Six 20mm
	Tubes Four 21in (1x4)
	AS Four DC throwers (replaced by Squid)
Machinery:	Geared turbines on two shafts giving
	40,000shp
Max speed:	36kts

CLASS NOTES

These, the final eight of the 1943 'C' class, were to the same design as the 'Ca' group, and were of all-welded construction.

HISTORICAL NOTES

HMS *Crown* never saw service in the Royal Navy, for although launched with that name, she was, upon completion, commissioned into the Royal Norwegian Navy.

HMS *Creole*, 'C' class Cr group, at anchor in 1946. (MoD (Navy))

HMS *Crispin*, 'C' class Cr group, at anchor in 1946. (MoD (Navy))

'BATTLE' CLASS

GROUP I

UNIT	COMMENCED	COMPLETED	BUILDER
Barfleur (leader)	1942	1944	Swan Hunter
Camperdown	1942	1945	Fairfield
Finisterre	1942	1945	Fairfield
Gabbard	1944	1946	Swan Hunter
Hogue	1943	1945	Cammell Laird
Lagos	1943	1945	Cammell Laird
St Kitts	1943	1946	Swan Hunter
Trafalgar (leader)	1943	1945	Swan Hunter

GROUP II

UNIT	COMMENCED	COMPLETED	BUILDER
Armada (leader)	1942	1945	Hawthorn Leslie
Cadiz	1943	1946	Fairfield
Gravelines	1943	1946	Cammell Laird
Saintes (leader)	1943	1946	Hawthorn Leslie
St James (leader)	1943	1946	Fairfield
Sluys	1943	1946	Cammell Laird
Solebay (leader)	1943	1945	Hawthorn Leslie
Vigo	1943	1946	Fairfield

Displacement:	2,315 tons (Group I)	*AA* Ten 40mm
	2,325 tons (Group II)	*Tubes* Eight 21in (2x4)
	3,250 tons (Group I full load)	*AS* Two DC throwers (replaced by one
	3,360 tons (Group II full load)	Squid)
Length:	379ft	**Machinery:** Geared turbines on two shafts giving
Breadth:	40ft	50,000shp
Draught:	12ft 9in	**Max speed:** 35.75kts
Armament:	*Main* Four 4.5in (2x2 in turrets)	

CLASS NOTES

This class was intended for service in the Tropics and the Pacific Theatre. They had the main armament forward and the anti-aircraft and light weapons aft of the funnel. The turrets were powered and the 4.5in guns had 85° elevation. The AA weapons were all mounted clear of the main deck.

Additionally a single 40mm Bofors was positioned aft of B turret in front of the bridge.

HMS *Saintes* was the trials vessel for the prototype 4.5in twin turret for the 'Daring' class.

Group I ships mounted a 4in for star shell aft of the funnel. These were not utility ships and took longer to build.

HMS *Gabbard*, 'Battle' class group I, at anchor in 1946. (MoD (Navy))

HMS *Hogue*, 'Battle' class group I, at sea with all armament and director trained to starboard. (Cammell Laird SB)

HMS *Sluys*, 'Battle' class group 2, leaving harbour in 1946. Note 4.5in aft of funnel and 40mm aft of the B turret before the bridge. (MoD (Navy))

LATER 'BATTLE' CLASS

UNIT	COMMENCED	COMPLETED	BUILDER
Agincourt (leader)	1943	1947	Hawthorn Leslie
Aisne	1943	1947	Vickers Armstrong (Tyne)
Alamein (leader)	1944	1948	Hawthorn Leslie
Barrosa	1943	1947	John Brown
Corunna (leader)	1944	1947	Swan Hunter
Dunkirk	1944	1946	Stephen
Jutland (ex-*Malplaquet*)	1944	1946	Stephen
Matapan (leader)	1944	1947	John Brown

HMS *Barrosa*, later 'Battle' class, entering harbour in 1947. (MoD (Navy))

Displacement:	2,640 tons (2,480 tons leaders)
	3,315 tons (full load) (3,375 tons leaders
	full load)
Armament:	*Main* Five 4.5in (2x2, 1x1)
	AA Eight 40mm
	Tubes Ten 21in (2x5)
	AS One triple Squid
Machinery:	Geared turbines on two shafts giving
	50,000shp
Max speed:	35.75kts

UNIT	BUILDER
Albuera	Vickers Armstrong (Tyne)
Belleisle	Fairfield
Mons	Hawthorn Leslie
*Namur**	Cammell Laird
Navarino	Cammell Laird
Omdurman	Fairfield
*Oudenarde**	Swan Hunter
Poictiers	Hawthorn Leslie
River Plate	Swan Hunter
St Lucia	Stephen
San Domingo	Cammell Laird
Somme	Cammell Laird
Talavera	Clydebank
Trincomalee	Clydebank
Waterloo	Fairfield
Vimiera	Not allocated
Ypres	Not allocated

Namur and *Oudenarde* were actually launched and made seaworthy, being expended later as targets.

CLASS NOTES

A very fine design of destroyer being an improved version of the 'Battle' class with greater firepower. An ideal recognition point for this class is the US style of 'pagoda battleship type' director just forward of the flag deck. None of this class saw Second World War service. All ships mounted a single 4.5in gun in shield aft of the funnel.

HISTORICAL NOTES

The following ships of both 'Battle' classes were in varying states of completion, some just a name on an order book, some on the slips, and some launched and fitting-out when the war ended. All were cancelled, broken up or scrapped.

HMS *Corunna*, later 'Battle' class, at sea in 1947. (MoD (Navy))

EX-GERMAN

'NARVIK' CLASS

Unit:	Nonsuch (ex-Z38)	Armament:	Main Five 5.9in
Commenced:	1942		AA Six 37mm, 16 20mm
Completed:	1943		Tubes Eight 21in
Builder:	Deschimag	Machinery:	Geared turbines on two shafts giving
Displacement:	2,650 tons (full load)		70,000shp
Length:	403ft 6in	Max speed:	35.5kts
Breadth:	38ft 6in	Fuel:	800 tons oil
Draught:	9ft 6in		

HMS *Nonsuch* (ex-German) 'Narvik' class, in harbour under German flag, 1944. (Real Photographs)

'MAASS' CLASS

Unit:	Z4 (ex-Richard Beitzon), Z10 (ex-Hans Lady)
Commended:	1935
Completed:	1941
Builder:	Z4 Deutsche werke
	Z10 Deschimag
Displacement:	1,625 tons
	2,360 tons (full load)
Length:	382ft
Breadth:	37ft 6in
Draught:	9ft 6in
Armament:	Main Five 5in
	AA Eight 37mm, 12 20mm
	Tubes Eight 21in
Machinery:	Geared turbines on two shafts giving 50,000shp
Max speed:	36kts

CLASS NOTES

These three ex-German destroyers were allocated to the Royal Navy as reparations after the war's end. They were taken to Portsmouth for evaluation and all three were made seaworthy – Z38 having a damaged hull and needing refit, Z10 had minor defects and Z4 had been badly damaged by a near miss from a bomb that took five months to repair. All carried sixty mines.

Z38 was commissioned as HMS *Nonsuch*, Z10 and Z4 were not used.

Z38 was one of the 'Narvik' class of destroyer built after the Battle of Narvik when the RN 'H' class gave battle to the prewar German destroyers in Narvik Fjord.

Z4 and Z10 were of the first German class to mount quadruple torpedo tubes in two mountings.

Although all three of these ships were on the Navy list, only HMS *Nonsuch* saw service under the White Ensign, being used as an air target towing vessel, being broken up in 1949.

'WEAPON' CLASS

UNIT	BUILDER
Battleaxe (leader)	Yarrow
Broadsword (leader)	Yarrow
Crossbow	Thornycroft
Scorpion (ex-*Tomahawk*, ex-*Centaur*)	White

Commenced:	1944
Completed:	1947 (*Broadsword* and *Crossbow* 1948)
Displacement:	2,000 tons
	2,835 tons (full load)
Length:	365ft
Breadth:	38ft
Draught:	12ft 9in
Armament:	*Main* Four 4in
	AA Four 40mm
	Tubes Ten 21in (2x5)
	AS 15 DCs carried, Two Squid
Machinery:	Geared turbines on two shafts giving 40,000shp
Max speed:	34kts

Left: HMS *Crossbow*, 'Weapon' class, entering harbour in 1959. (MoD (Navy))

Below: HMS *Broadsword*, 'Weapon' class, at anchor in 1948. (MoD (Navy))

CLASS NOTES

This class was composed of destroyers intended for fleet use but altered at design stage for anti-submarine work, and thus only mounted four instead of six 4in guns. In the first two ships the 4in guns were in A and X positions, in the latter two, in A and B positions; all the 4in guns were in shields.

These were the first two-funnelled destroyers to be built since the 'Tribals' of 1939 and the only completed units from a planned total of twenty.

The outline was similar to the next class, the 'Darings'. The fore funnel was built inside the lattice foremast and all were fitted as leaders. This class design was an enlargement of the 'Hunt' Type IV.

HISTORICAL NOTES

HMS *Carronade* of this class was launched but not completed.

HMS *Scorpion* was the destroyer chosen to be the trials ship for the Limbo anti-submarine weapon.

'DARING' CLASS

UNIT	COMMENCED	COMPLETED	BUILDER
Dainty	1945	1953	White
Daring	1945	1952	Swan Hunter
Decoy (ex-Dragon)	1946	1953	Yarrow
Defender (ex-Dogstar)	1949	1952	Stephen
Delight (ex-Disdain, ex-Ypres)	1946	1953	Fairfield
Diamond	1947	1954	John Brown
Diana (ex-Druid)	1947	1954	John Brown
Duchess	1948	1952	Thornycroft

Displacement:	2,610 tons
	3,600 tons (full load)
Length:	390ft
Breadth:	43ft
Draught:	12ft 9in
Armament:	*Main* Six 4.5in (3x2 in turrets)
	AA Six 40mm
	Tubes Ten 21in (2x5)
	AS Squid
Machinery:	Geared turbines on two shafts giving
	54,000shp
Max speed:	34.75kts

CLASS NOTES

This class is a partial design improvement on the 'Battle' and 'Weapon' classes, and of all-welded construction. A recognition feature is the bridge of new design, also the 4.5in gun turrets. The fore funnel is partly built into and concealed by the foremast.

All classed as leaders, sixteen were planned.

The 'Daring' class destroyers have been described as 'super destroyers' and even as 'ultralight cruisers'. Up to the year 1954, they were the largest destroyers in size and tonnage in the RN.

HMS *Daring*, 'Daring' class, at sea in 1952. Note smoke from fore funnel. (MoD (Navy))

HMS *Delight*, 'Daring' class, at anchor in 1953. (MoD (Navy))

'COUNTY' CLASS

UNIT	COMMENCED	COMPLETED	BUILDER
Antrim	1966	1971	Fairfield
Devonshire	1959	1962	Cammell Laird
Fife	1962	1966	Vickers Armstrong (Tyne)
Glamorgan	1962	1966	Fairfield
Hampshire	1959	1963	John Brown (Clyde)
Kent	1960	1963	Harland & Wolff
London	1960	1963	Swan Hunter
Norfolk	1966	1970	Swan Hunter

Displacement:	5,200 tons
	6,200 tons (full load)
Length:	520ft 6in
Breadth:	54ft
Draught:	20ft
Armament:	*Main* Four 4.5in (2x2 in turrets)
	AA Two 20mm
	Missiles Two quadruple Seacat, One
	Seaslug (twin mounting)
	Tubes Three 12.75in (either beam if fitted)
Machinery:	Combined steam and gas, COSAG, on
	two shafts giving 60,000shp
Max speed:	32.5kts
Range:	3,500 miles at 28kts

HMS *Devonshire*, 'County' class, on builder's trials under the Red Ensign, 1962. (MoD (Navy))

CLASS NOTES

These eight ships when built embodied the latest technological developments enabling them to fight in a nuclear war. Armed with Seaslug and Seacat surface-to-surface and surface-to-air missiles, the 'County' class had a powerful anti-ship armament not forgetting the four 4.5in guns which are semi-automatic, dual-purpose and have a good angle of elevation. Anti-submarine warfare is taken care of by the ship's flight of one or two Wessex helicopters and the AS torpedoes, which are also light enough for helicopter use and carry an 88lb warhead. Other defensive equipment includes two eight-barrelled Corvus chaff-dischargers which dispense a screen of chaff to obscure the ship to enemy missiles. The launchers are mounted port and starboard of the fore funnel. The engine room has one AEI and one G6 turbine on each shaft. The machinery is similar to that on the Type 81 'Tribal' class frigates.

TYPE 82

Unit:	*Bristol*	**Armament:**	*Main* One Sea Dart (twin mounting in Y position)
Builder:	Associated Shipbuilders, Wallsend-on-Tyne		One 4.5in (turret in A position)
Commenced:	Nov 1967		*AA* Two 20 mm (2x1)
Completed:	Dec 1972		*AS* Ikara aft A position, Limbo Mk 10 (One three-barrel mounting)
Displacement:	5,650 tons	**Machinery:**	COSAG on two shafts developing 74,600shp
	6,750 tons (full load)		
Length:	508ft	**Max speed:**	28kts
Breadth:	55ft	**Range:**	5,000nm at 18kts
Draught:	22ft 6in	**Helicopter:**	Deck suitable for Wasp, no hangar

HMS *Bristol*, Type 82, at sea on builder's trials in 1975. (MoD (Navy))

CLASS NOTES

HMS *Bristol* is the only completed example of an aircraft carrier escort vessel. A total of eight was proposed but only this example, ordered in October 1966, was commissioned. She has stabilisers and all her compartments are air conditioned. She is the only three-funnelled ship in the Royal Navy.

TYPE 42

UNIT	COMMENCED	COMPLETED	BUILDER
Birmingham	1971	1976	Cammell Laird
Cardiff	1971	1978	Vickers-Barrow
Coventry	1972	1978	Cammell Laird
Exeter	1976	1978	Swan Hunter
Glasgow	1972	1978	Swan Hunter
Liverpool	1978	1982	Cammell Laird
Newcastle	1972	1978	Swan Hunter
Nottingham	1978	1982	Vosper Thornycroft
Sheffield	1970	1974	Vickers-Barrow
Southampton	1978	1981	Vosper Thornycroft

Displacement:	3,150 tons		*Tubes* Six 12.75in AS (2x3 abreast of
	4,100 tons (full load)		after director)
Length:	410ft	Machinery:	COGOG on two shafts giving 50,000
Breadth:	46ft		and 8,000shp
Draught:	19ft	Max speed:	28kts
Armament:	*Main* Twin Sea Dart Mk 30 (in B position)	Range:	650nm at 30kts
	One 4.5in (turret in A position)		4,500nm at 18kts
	AA Two 20mm (2x1)	Helicopter:	One Lynx armed with Sea Skua

HMS *Sheffield*, 'Towns' class, leaving Vickers basin for sea trials. (Vickers)

CLASS NOTES

A simpler design of warship than HMS *Bristol*, but in general based on the Type 82 specification. The high speed Olympus turbines are not coupled to the Tyne turbines which are only used for cruising. Each shaft has a five-bladed variable pitch propeller. HMS *Sheffield* was ordered in November 1968.

The 4.5in gun has depression of 10° and elevation of 55° from the horizontal, with twenty-five rounds/barrel/min. The weight of the shell (HE charge) is 21kg, and its range 22km. This weapon is developed from the Abbot SP gun.

The Sea Dart missile is propelled by a solid fuel booster engine and a ramjet sustainer with radar guidance. The missile is semi-active radar homed, with an HE warhead and a range of 25nm.

The Sea Skua missile is propelled by solid fuel rocket and guided by radar and/or radio control with an estimated maximum effective range of 6nm and carries an HE warhead of 45lb.

The 12.75in-diameter torpedo is an active and/or acoustic homing weapon, mainly for air-to-surface/sub-surface warfare.

HISTORICAL NOTES

HMS *Sheffield*: after attack by Argentinian aircraft was hit by an Exocet missile when north of West Falkland on 4 May 1982 and caught fire, having to be abandoned, and sank on 10 May 1982.

HMS *Coventry*: after an aircraft attack during which she was heavily bombed, sank on 25 May 1982 north of the Falkland Sound.

HMS *Birmingham*, 'Towns' class, at sea. (MoD (Navy))

HMS *Newcastle*, 'Towns' class, at sea under the Red Ensign for builder's trials. (MoD (Navy))

IMPROVED TYPE 42

UNIT	COMMENCED	COMPLETED	BUILDER
Edinburgh	1980	1985	Cammell Laird
Gloucester	1979	1984	Vosper Thornycroft
Manchester	1978	1982	Vickers-Barrow
York	1980	1985	Swan Hunter

Displacement:	4,775 tons (full load 5,380 tons)		tubes (2x3) with Mk 44 torpedoes for helicopter use.
Dimensions:	462.75ft x 49ft x 19ft		
Armament:	*Main* Twin Sea Dart Mk 30 (in B position)	**Machinery:**	COGOG on two shafts giving 56,000 and 8,100 shp
	One 4.5in Mk 8 DP automatic piece (in A position)	**Speed:**	30+ knots
	AA Four 30mm (2x2), four 20mm	**Range:**	4,000nm at 18 knots
	(4x1); however the weapon outfit varies	**Fuel:**	600 tons of oil fuel
	throughout.	**Complement:**	301
	Tubes Two STWS Mk 46 torpedo	**Helicopter:**	One Lynx Mk 2 normally armed with the Sea Skua anti-ship missile

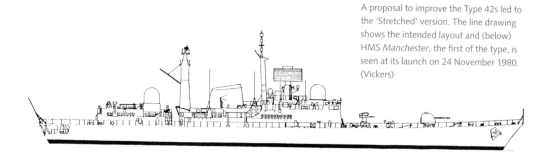

A proposal to improve the Type 42s led to the 'Stretched' version. The line drawing shows the intended layout and (below) HMS *Manchester*, the first of the type, is seen at its launch on 24 November 1980. (Vickers)

HMS *Manchester* in a tight port turn. (MoD (Navy))

NOTES

All similar to the basic Type 42 Class but are 2ft additional beam and 42ft additional length. Built with twin rudders, variable pitch propellers and two pairs of stabilisers.

Missile magazine capacity enables forty Sea Dart to be stored as against twenty-four in Type 42 ships and the small-calibre AA armament has been increased as a result of the South Atlantic campaign of 1982.

HMS *Gloucester* wearing her pennant on harbour evolutions. (MoD (Navy))

'DARING' CLASS TYPE 45 DESTROYERS

Building by Vosper-Thornycroft. Vickers (Barrow), Yarrow SB; all being BAE Systems.

HMS	COMMENCED	COMPLETED
Daring	2003	2007
Dauntless	2004	2009
Defender	2006	2010
Diamond	2004	2009
Dragon	2005	2010
Duncan	2006	2011

Note: Estimated year in service will be one year later than completed year.

Type 45, HMS *Diamond*. (Fleet Photographic, MoD)

Dispacement:	7,350 tons (5,801 tons full load)
Dimensions:	500ft x 69.5ft x 16.5ft
Armament:	One 4.5in Mk 8 Mod.1, range 14nm
	AA gun – two Phalanx (P&S)
	Two 30mm (P&S)
	Missiles Bow silo with ASTER 15/30 (SAM)
	SEA SKUA for helicopter use (SSM)
	Tubes Fitted for Mk 2 STINGRAY (P&S)
	Decoys Four SEAGNAT
Machinery:	Two shaft connected to gas turbine 28,000shp and diesel 26,800bhp (Rolls-Royce and Grumman)
Speed (trial):	31½kts (29kts sea speed)
Range:	7,000nm at 18kts
Aircraft:	Lynx or Merlin
Complement:	187 peace with additional sixty berths for Royal Marines etc.

NOTES

A large tonnage vessel with modern electronics, the closest RN fighting ships of recent times have been County HMS *Devonshire*, Type 42 HMS *Manchester* Mk 3 and Type 22 Batch 3 as HMS *Cornwall* (the largest frigates in any navy). Possible updates could be the 5.75in gun and fitting of cruise missiles, e.g. EXOCET or HARPOON or similar.

It should be noted that the average destroyer of the Second World War had 40,000shp with four 4.7in or 4.5in guns plus eight 21in torpedoes on two quad mtgs.

Above: Type 45, HMS *Daring*. (Fleet Photographic, MoD)

Right: Type 45, HMS *Dauntless*. (Fleet Photographic, MoD)

APPENDIX 1

Destroyer Armament

Guns

Calibre	Muzzle Velocity (ft/sec)	Projectile weight	Notes
6in	2,400	100lb	As mounted on HMS *Swift*, 1917, only. Never fitted again.
4.7in DP	3,000	55–65lb	QF – Mounted on the majority of classes from the Thornycroft leaders of 1917.
4.5in DP	3,750	60lb	QF – First mounted in the 'Z' class 1943. In the latest classes are automatic.
4in DP	2,300	31lb or 25lb	QF – The main armament of destroyers from the 'F' class 1908 and for many vessels in the Second World War.
3in or 12pdr	2,500	12–16lb	Mounted on the first 'A' to 'E' classes and usually referred to as 12-pounders.
2.24in	1,740	6lb	As above and known as 6-pounders.
'Pom-Poms'	2,000	2lb	First effectively used in the Boer War on land. Fully automatic action.
40mm Bofors	2,500	4.5lb	One of the best light AA pieces designed. Fully automatic action.
20mm Oerlikon	2,725	125g	A heavy machine-gun weapon for short-range AA work.
.5in Vickers	2,520	2.19oz	Heavy machine-gun type. Chiefly for short-range AA work.

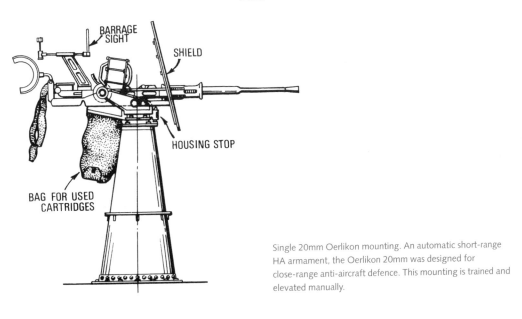

BARRAGE SIGHT

SHIELD

HOUSING STOP

BAG FOR USED CARTRIDGES

Single 20mm Oerlikon mounting. An automatic short-range HA armament, the Oerlikon 20mm was designed for close-range anti-aircraft defence. This mounting is trained and elevated manually.

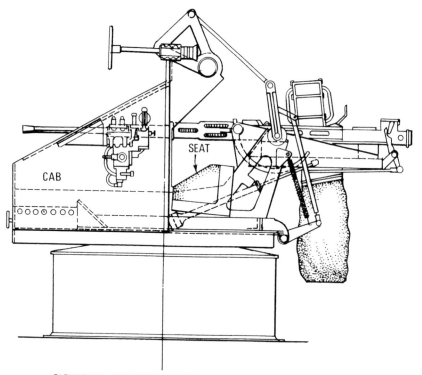

ELEVATION OF GUNLAYERS SIDE OF TWIN MOUNTING

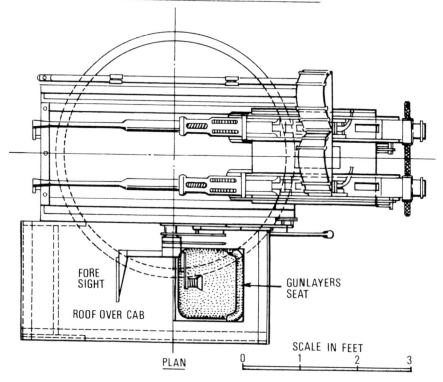

PLAN

SCALE IN FEET

Elevation and plan views of a twin 20mm Oerlikon mounting. With power-operated traverse and elevation, the effective range of this weapon was 1,000yd.

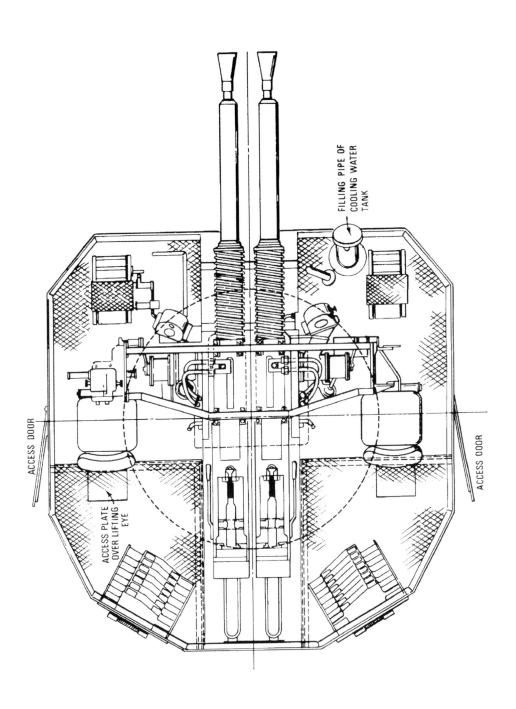

Plan view of a twin 40mm Bofors medium-range HA mounting, showing director's and trainer's seats and chequer plate for the loading numbers to maintain their foothold in heavy seas.

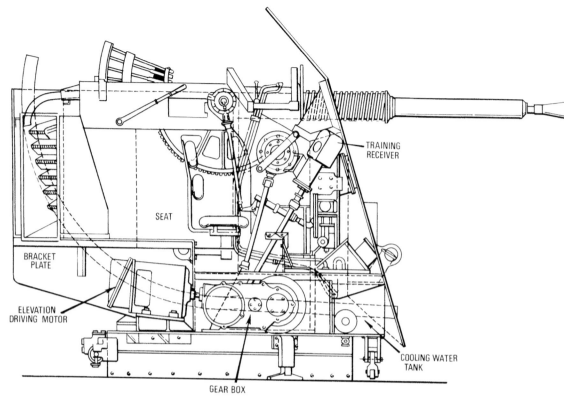

Elevation of a twin 40mm Bofors. This mounting was a logical extension of the single piece seen below, with the advantage of complete automation for elevation and training, but full local control independent of the director when necessary.

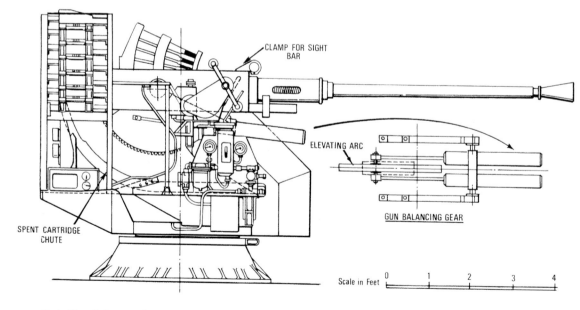

Single 40mm Bofors mounting. Power-operated for training and elevation, local control is built into this weapon.

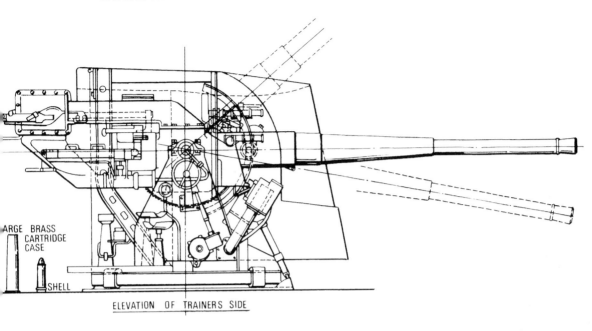

LARGE BRASS
CARTRIDGE
CASE

SHELL

ELEVATION OF TRAINERS SIDE

4.7in QF Mk IX gun on the CP Mk XVIII mounting. It has an elevation of 40° and depression of 10°. The gun itself is built up of three forgings – the gun tube (called the 'A' tube), the jacket and the breech ring.

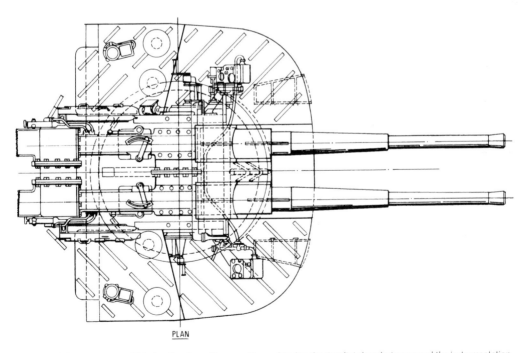

PLAN

Plan view of the 4.7in DP gun. This drawing shows the mounting as fitted to the 'Javelin' class destroyers and the instrumentation for training, elevation and fuse setting in either local or director control.

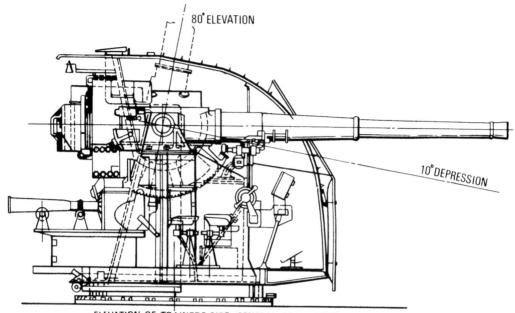

80° ELEVATION

10° DEPRESSION

ELEVATION OF TRAINERS SIDE GENERAL ARRANGEMENT

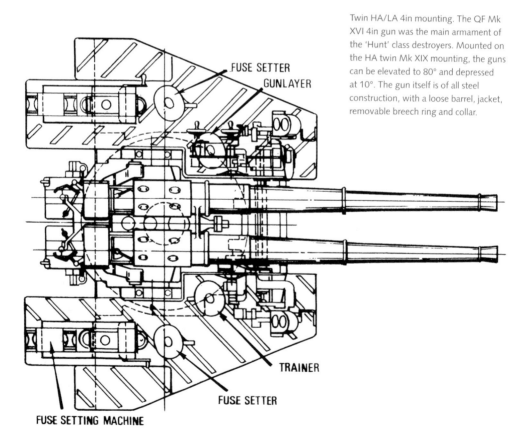

FUSE SETTER
GUNLAYER

TRAINER

FUSE SETTER

FUSE SETTING MACHINE

Twin HA/LA 4in mounting. The QF Mk XVI 4in gun was the main armament of the 'Hunt' class destroyers. Mounted on the HA twin Mk XIX mounting, the guns can be elevated to 80° and depressed at 10°. The gun itself is of all steel construction, with a loose barrel, jacket, removable breech ring and collar.

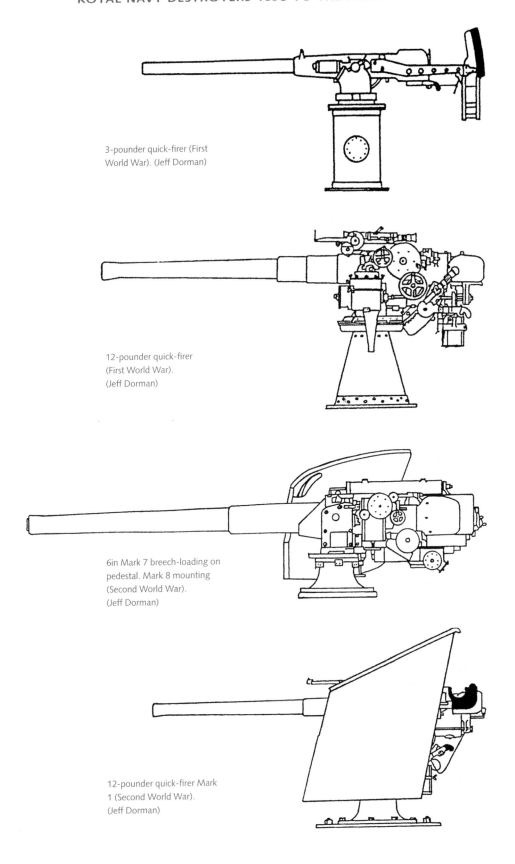

3-pounder quick-firer (First
World War). (Jeff Dorman)

12-pounder quick-firer
(First World War).
(Jeff Dorman)

6in Mark 7 breech-loading on
pedestal. Mark 8 mounting
(Second World War).
(Jeff Dorman)

12-pounder quick-firer Mark
1 (Second World War).
(Jeff Dorman)

Anti-Submarine Weapons

Name	Description	Notes
Depth Charge	300lb charge in an oil-drum-shaped cylindrical container. Detonates at a preset depth. In the Second World War a cast-iron ballast weight was fitted to give a fast sink rate.	Brought into service between 1914–18. Either fired abeam from a mortar-like thrower, or released from a chute by gravity.
Hedgehog	24 spigot-type bombs mounted upon a rectangular cradle, forward of the bridge, and fired ahead on a given command, in an oval pattern; the bombs had a 37lb charge with contact fuse.	In service from 1942 and later. Range: 1 cable; effective down to 1,250ft.
Squid	Two, three or four bombs fired from barrels, similar to the mortar principle. Bombs of 500lb charge.	Not in service in the RN today. Range: 3 cables.
Limbo Mk 10	As mortar with all round coverage, has three barrels. Maximum effective range of 5 cables.	In service today. Introduced in the early 1960s as an improved Squid.

Practice drill at a depth charge thrower on board HMS *Anthony* ('A' class) during the interwar years. (IWM)

Guided Missiles

Name	Description	Notes
Seaslug	Medium-range AA missile with surface-to-surface capability. 15 miles range, 500–50,000ft altitude.	Used in the 'County' class, after trials in HMS *Girdle Ness*. Mk I and II fitted.
Sea Dart	Medium-range DP missile up to 25 miles and between 100–60,000ft altitude.	Fitted in HMS *Bristol* and Type 42 'Sheffield' class.
Seacat	Short-range AA missile with DP possibility, range/height 13,000ft.	Fitted in the majority of RN fighting ships.
Sea Skua	This is a comparatively new missile launched from the helicopter for anti-ship use.	
Harpoon	A tactical surface-to-surface missile system with a range of 55–120nm. Missile particulars are: length 15ft, weight 1,470lb, speed Mach 0.9, warhead 500lb HE or nuclear. Propulsion is by solid fuel rocket motor and guidance is by radar.	Likely to be fitted to the Type 42s.

Sea Slug. This medium-range ship-to-air missile is fitted in the 'County' class guided missile destroyers, in this case HMS *Kent*. It has four solid propellant boosters which jettison after burn-out. It is guided by a beam riding system from radar Type 901. (MoD (Navy))

Above: Sea Dart. This medium-range ship-to-air missile is propelled by ramjets. It also has an anti-ship capability. (MoD (Navy))

Right: Seacat. A highly efficient close-range anti-aircraft missile which can be used in a surface-to-surface role. Guidance is by radio control with solid fuel propulsion. (MoD (Navy))

Lynx helicopter with two Mk 44/46 torpedoes. Developed for AS and other duties, the Lynx carries a variety of armaments including the Sea Skua semi-active homing missile. The Lynx is carried by the Type 42s. (Fleet Air Arm Museum)

Wasp helicopter used in conjunction with the Type 81s, normally armed with two Mk 44/46 torpedoes. (Fleet Air Arm Museum)

Merlin EH101 ASW helicopter. (Westland Helicopters)

The Sea King helicopter carries a variety of equipment including sonar, search radar and up to four Mk 44 torpedoes or depth charges. (Fleet Air Arm Museum)

Wessex helicopter, normally carried on 'County' class destroyers. (Fleet Air Arm Museum)

Torpedoes

Name	Description	Notes
14in	Used in the earliest TBDs up to the Admiralty 'S' Class.	Either the tube mounting or ship, or both had to be 'trained' for the torpedo to bear directly at the target
18in	Used in the 'B' to 'F' classes.	
21in	Classes after the 'S' class up to the 'County' class of 1960.	
12.75in	This is a recent type of torpedo being electrically propelled and with a warhead of only 88lb. It is much shorter than the 21in torpedo and is ideal for helicopter use.	Provided for the 'County' and later classes.

21in torpedo test firing from HMS *Broke*, c.1914. (Vickers)

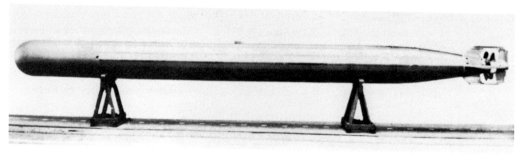

18in torpedo-less pistol arming device on warhead. (Vickers)

21in torpedo clearing the deck of a destroyer into the sea. (IWM)

Guns as used for Fortification but as Fitted to HM Destroyers

3in quick-firing, 12-pounder DP gun at Smethwick Drill Hall. (Dr M. Osborne)

12-pounder QF at Weybourne Camp, Norfolk. (Dr M. Osborne)

12-pounder QF at Tilbury Fort. (Dr M. Osborne)

12-pounder gun at Tilbury
Fort Coastal Defence.
First World War.
(Dr M. Osborne)

12-pounder coastal defence
gun at Pendennis.
(Dr M. Osborne)

Hotchkiss 6-pounder coast
defence gun at Tilbury Fort.
(Dr M. Osborne)

APPENDIX 2

Destroyer Builders in the UK

Cammell Laird & Co. (Shipbuilders and Engineers) Ltd, Birkenhead, Cheshire.
John Brown & Co. (Shipbuilders and Engineers) Ltd, Clydebank, Glasgow.
Wm Denny & Bros Ltd, Dumbarton.
The Fairfield Shipbuilding & Engineering Co. Ltd, Govan, Glasgow.
Harland & Wolff Ltd, Belfast, Glasgow and Govan.
R. & W. Hawthorn Leslie & Co. Ltd, Hebburn-on-Tyne.
Scotts Shipbuilding & Engineering Co. Ltd (Greenock).
Smiths Dock Co. Ltd, South Bank on Tees.
Alex, Stephen & Sons Ltd (Linthouse, Govan, Glasgow).
Swan Hunter & Wigham Richardson Ltd, Wallsend-on-Tyne.
John I. Thornycroft & Co. Ltd, Woolston, Southampton.
Vickers-Armstrong, Naval Yard, Barrow-in-Furness, Lancashire.
Vickers-Armstrong, Naval Yard, High Walker, Newcastle upon Tyne, and Palmers Hebburn Co. Ltd.
J. Samuel White & Co. Ltd, Cowes.
Yarrow & Co. Ltd, Scotstoun, Glasgow.

Also used: Doxford (Sunderland); Earle (Hull); Harland & Wolff (Clyde); Inglis (Clyde); Thames Ironworks (Blackwall); Beardmore (Clyde).

APPENDIX 3

Details of Torpedo Catchers and Torpedo Destroyers

Unit	Length (ft)	Speed (kts)	Armament	Completed
Alarm	230	17	2-12pdr and 4 smallbore	1892
Antelope	230	17	2-12pdr and 4 smallbore	c.1892
Assaye	230	15	2-12pdr and 4 smallbore	1891
Barracouta	220	14	6-12pdr and 4 smallbore	1889
Barrossa	220	14	6-12pdr and 4 smallbore	1889
Blanche	220	14	6-12pdr and 4 smallbore	1889
Blonde	230	14	6-12pdr and 4 smallbore	1892
Boomerang	230	15	2-12pdr and 4 smallbore	1892
Circe	230	17	2-12pdr and 4 smallbore	1892
Curlew	195	10	1-6in and 3-4.7in	1885
Dryad	250	16.5	2-12pdr and 4 smallbore	1890
Fearless	220	12	4-12pdr and 8 smallbore 1 submerged TT	1886
Gleaner	230	15	2-12pdr and 4 smallbore	1890
Gossamer	230	15	2-12pdr and 4 smallbore	1890
Grasshopper	200	?	6 smallbore	1887
Halcyon	250	16.5	2-12pdr and 4 smallbore	c.1890
Harrier	250	16.5	2-12pdr and 4 smallbore	c.1890
Hazard	250	16.5	2-12pdr and 4 smallbore	c.1890
Hebe	230	17	2-12pdr and 4 smallbore	1892
Hussar	250	16.5	2-12pdr and 4 smallbore	c.1890
Jason	230	17	2-12pdr and 4 smallbore	1892
Jaseur	230	17	2-12pdr and 4 smallbore	1892
Karrakatta	230	15	2-12pdr and 4 smallbore	1889
Landrail	195	10	1-6in and 3-4.7in	1886
Leda	230	17	2-12pdr and 4 smallbore	1892
Niger	230	17	2-12pdr and 4 smallbore	1892
Onyx	230	17	2-12pdr and 4 smallbore	1892
Peassey	230	15	2-12pdr and 4 smallbore	1890
Rattlesnake	200	17.5	1-12pdr and 6 smallbore	1886
Salamander	230	15	2-12pdr and 4 smallbore	1889
Sandfly	200	?	6 smallbore	1887
Scout	220	12	4-12pdr and 8 smallbore and 1 submerged TT	1885

Unit	Length (ft)	Speed (kts)	Armament	Completed
Seagull	230	15	2-12pdr and 4 smallbore	1889
Sharpshooter	230	18	2-12pdr and 4 smallbore	1888
Sheldrake	230	15	2-12pdr and 4 smallbore	1889
Skipjack	230	15	2-12pdr and 4 smallbore	1889
Spanker	230	15	2-12pdr and 4 smallbore	1889
Speedwell	230	15	2-12pdr and 4 smallbore	1889
Spider	200	?	1-12pdr and 6 smallbore	1887

APPENDIX 4

Statement of Losses of HM Destroyers and Torpedo Boats

Torpedo Boats Lost 1914–18

HMTB 9 (ex-HMTB *Grasshopper*) was lost by collision in the North Sea, 24 July 1916.

HMTB 10 (ex-HMTB *Greenfly*) was torpedoed by a U-boat in the North Sea 10 June 1915.

HMTB 11 (ex-HMTB *Moth*) struck a mine off the east coast, 7 March 1916.

HMTB 12 (ex-HMTB *Mayfly*) was torpedoed by a U-boat in the North Sea on 10 June 1915.

HMTB 13 was lost by collision in the North Sea, 28 January 1916.

HMTB 24 was wrecked off Dover Harbour breakwater. 28 January 1917.

HMTB 46 foundered in a storm in the eastern Mediterranean on 27 December 1915.

HMTB 64 was wrecked in the Aegean sea on 21 March 1915.

HMTB 90 capsized in a storm off Gibraltar on 25 April 1918.

HMTB 96 collided with a Mercantile Fleet Auxillary off Gibraltar on 1 November 1915.

HMTB 17 was lost by collision in the English Channel, 10 June 1917.

SUMMARY

Foundered:	4
Collision:	4
Mined:	1
Torpedoed:	2
Total:	11

At the cessation of hostilities in 1918 HMTB 1–8, 14–23, 25–36 and 116 were still in service.

Torpedo Boat Destroyers Lost 1914–18

Ardent, Ariel, Arno, Attack, Bittern, Boxer, Cheerful, Comet, Contest, Coquette, Derwent, Eden, Erne, Fairy, Falcon, Flirt, Fortune, Foyle, Goldfinch, Gurkha, Hoste, Itchen, Kale, Laforey, Lassoo, Lightning, Louis, Lynx, Maori, Marmion, Mary Rose, Medusa, Myrmidon, Narborough, Negro, Nessus, Nestor, Nomad, North Star, Nubian*, Opal, Paragon, Partridge, Pheasant, Phoenix, Pincher, Racoon, Recruit (1), Recruit (2), Scott, Setter, Shark, Simoon, Sparrowhawk, Staunch, Strongbow, Success, Surprise, Tipperary, Tornado, Torrent, Turbulent, Ulleswater, Ulysses, Vehement, Velox, Vittoria**, Wolverine, Zulu*.

SUMMARY

Mined:	22
Sunk by U-boat:	10 (see details below)
Rammed:	2
Surface action:	13
Collision:	14
Wrecked:	8
Total:	69

*   *Nubian* and *Zulu* were only counted as one loss, see page 27.

** *Vittoria* was not lost during the war, see page 49.

RN Destroyers Lost by Enemy Submarine Attack 1914–18

Attacked	By	Nationality	Attacked	By	Nationality
Attack	UC34	German	Recruit (2)	UB16	German
Comet	Unknown	Austrian	Scott	UC17	German
Contest	Unknown	German	Staunch	UC38	German
Fairy	UC75	German	Ulleswater	Unknown	German
Itchen	U99	German			
Phoenix	UXXVII	Austrian			
Recruit (1)	Unknown	German			

Lassoo, Surprise, Tornado and Torrent were mined and not lost by U-boat torpedo.

RN Destroyers Lost 1939–45

Acasta, Achates, Acheron, Afridi, Airedale, Aldenham, Ardent, Basilisk, Bath, Bedouin, Belmont, Berkeley, Beverley, Blanche, Blean, Boadicea, Brazen, Broadwater, Broke, Campbeltown, Cameron, Codrington, Cossack, Dainty, Daring, Defender, Deiatelnyi (ex-Churchill), Delight, Diamond, Duchess, Dulverton, Eclipse, Electra, Encounter, Escort, Esk, Eskdale, Exmoor, Exmouth, Fearless, Firedrake, Foresight, Fury, Gallant, Gipsy, Glowworm, Grafton, Grenade, Grenville, Greyhound, Grove, Gurkha (1), Gurkha (2) (ex-Larne), Hardy (1), Hardy (2), Harvester, Hasty, Havant, Havock, Hereward, Heythrop, Holcombe, Hostile, Hunter, Hurricane, Hurworth, Hyperion, Imogen, Imperial, Inglefield, Intrepid, Isis, Ivanhoe, Jackal, Jaguar, Janus, Jersey, Juno, Jupiter, Khandahar, Khashmir, Keith, Kelly, Khartoum, Kingston, Kipling, Kujawiak (ex-Oakley (1)), La Combattante (ex-Haldon), Laforey, Lance, Legion, Lightning, Limbourne, Lively, Mahratta, Maori, Martin, Mashona, Matabele, Mohawk, Nestor, Orkan (ex-Myrmidon), Pakenham, Panther, Partridge, Penylan, Puckeridge, Punjabi, Quail, Quentin, Quorn, Rockingham, Sikh, Somali, Southwold, Stanley, Stronghold, Sturdy, Svenner (ex-Shark), Swift, Tenedos, Thanet, Tynedale, Valentine, Vampire, Venetia, Veteran, Vimiera, Vortigern, Wakeful, Warwick, Waterhen, Wessex, Whirlwind, Whitley, Wild Swan, Wren, Wrestler, Wryneck, Zulu.

SUMMARY

Mind:	23
Aircraft attack:	50
Sunk by U-boat:	36 (see details below)
Surface action:	20
Shore batteries:	2
Collision:	3
Wrecked:	2
Blockship:	1
Accident:	1
Uncertain:	2
Total:	140

RN Destroyers Lost by Enemy Submarine Attack 1939–45

Attacked	By	Nationality	Attacked	By	Nationality
Bath	U201	German	Grove	U77	German
Belmont	U82	German	Gurkha (2)	U133	German
Beverley	U188	German	Hardy (2)	U278	German
Blean	U443	German	Harvester	U432	German
Broadwater	U101	German	Heythrop	U652	German
Cossack	U563	German	Holcombe	U593	German
Daring	U23	German	Hurricane	U415	German
Churchill (later Deiatelnyi)	U956	German	Hyperion	Serpente	Italian
			Jaguar	U652	German
Escort	Marconi	Italian	Laforey	U223	German
Exmouth	U22	German	Mahratta	U956	German
Firedrake	U211	German	Martin	U431	German

Views of HMS *Saumarez* and HMS *Volage* after mining in 1946. Both struck mines in the international waters of the Corfu Channel. Both received great damage and HMS *Volage* had her bows blown off. (Both: J. Wilkinson)

Attacked	By	Nationality	Attacked	By	Nationality
Matabele	U454	German	*Veteran*	U404	German
Myrmidon	U610	German	*Warwick*	U413	German
(later *Orkan*)			*Whirlwind*	U34	German
Partridge	U565	German			
Puckeridge	U617	German			
Somali	U703	German			
Stanley	U574	German			
Tynedale	U593	German			

Destroyer casualties caused by either Italian or German weapons similar to the Chariots and X-Craft of the Royal Navy are not included in this appendix.

Torpedo Boat Destroyers and Destroyers Lost in Time of Peace

Ariel, 'D' class, was wrecked on the breakwater at Ricasoli whilst testing harbour defences on 19 April 1907.

Battleaxe, 'Weapon' class, was a constructive total loss after collision with HMS *Ursa* in the Clyde Estuary on 2 August 1962.

Blackwater, 'E' class, sank after colliding with the SS *Hero* on 6 April 1909 off Dungeness.

Cleveland, 'Hunt' Type 1, whilst on passage off Swansea on 28 June 1957 was stranded and became a total loss, being finally blown up on 14 December 1959.

Cobra, 'C' class, went ashore near Cromer, on 19 September 1901.

Decoy, 'A' class, sank on 13 August 1904 after colliding with HMS *Arun* off the Wolf Rock.

Gala, 'E' class, sank after colliding with HMS *Attentive* off Harwich.

Hogue, 'Battle' class, was a constructive total loss after collision with the Indian cruiser *Mysore* off Ceylon on 28 May 1959.

Lee, 'C' class, was wrecked on 5 October 1909 near Blacksod Bay.

Salmon, 'A' class, sank on 2 December 1901 after colliding with SS *Cambridge* at Harwich.

Sparrowhawk, 'B' class, was wrecked on 17 June 1904 at the mouth of the Yangtse River.

Speedy, Thornycroft 'S' class, sank on 24 December 1922 after colliding with a tug in the Sea of Marmora.

Stonehenge, Admiralty 'S' class, was wrecked on 6 November 1920 off Smyrna.

Tiger, 'E' class, sank on 2 April 1908 after colliding with HMS *Berwick* off St Catherines.

Viper, 'C' class, went aground on Bushan Island off Alderney on 3 August 1901.

Walrus, Admiralty 'V' class, was wrecked on 12 February 1938 in Filey Bay, refloated 29 March and broken up in October 1938.

SUMMARY

Collision:	6
Wrecked:	8
Total:	14

APPENDIX 5

Enemy Submarines and Ships Mainly Sunk by RN Destroyers

German Submarines 1914–18

U-boat	Date of Attack	Details
U8	4 March 1915	HMS *Gurkha* and *Maori* in the Straits of Dover.
U12	10 March 1915	HMS *Ariel* by ramming off Aberdeen.
U48	24 November 1917	HMS *Gipsy* (also spelt *Gypsy*) and five of HM trawlers by shellfire, U48 being stranded on the Goodwin Sands.
U69	12 July 1917	HMS *Patriot* in the North Sea.
UB29	6 December 1916	HMS *Ariel*, 12 miles south-west of the Bishop Rock Lighthouse.
UB70	8 May 1918	HMS *Basilisk*, and the USS *Sydonia* off Malta.
UB110	19 July 1918	HMS *Garry*, north-west of Spurn Point being later raised and salvaged by the RN.
UC16	23 October 1917	HMS *Melampus*, off Selsey Bill.
UC19	4 December 1916	HMS *Llewellyn* in the Straits of Dover.
UC26	9 May 1917	HMS *Milne*, by ramming in the Thames Estuary.
UC46	8 December 1917	HMS *Liberty*, by ramming in the Straits of Dover.
UC50	4 February 1918	HMS *Zubian*, by ramming in the North Sea.
UC75	31 May 1918	HMS *Fairy*, by ramming in the North Sea.

German Submarines 1939–45

U-boat	Date of Attack	Details
U27	22 September 1939	HMS *Forester* and *Fortune* west of the Hebrides.
U31	2 November 1940	HMS *Anthony* in the North Atlantic. (U31 had been previously sunk on 11 March 1940 by Allied aircraft in the Schilling Roads. She was raised, refitted and recommissioned.)
U32	30 October 1940	HMS *Harvester* and *Highlander* in the North Atlantic.
U35	29 November 1939	HMS *Icarus*, *Kashmir* and *Kingston* north-west of Bergen.
U39	14 September 1939	HMS *Faulknor*, *Firedrake* and *Foxhound*, north-west coast of N. Ireland.
U41	5 February 1940	HMS *Antelope* off the southern coast of Ireland.
U42	13 October 1939	HMS *Ilex* and *Imogen* off the southern coast of Ireland.
U44	20 March 1940	HMS *Fortune* off the north coast of Shetland.
U45	14 October 1939	HMS *Inglefield*, *Intrepid* and *Ivanhoe* off the coast of Ireland.
U49	15 April 1940	HMS *Fearless* off Narvik.
U50	10 April 1940	HMS *Hero* off the north coast of Shetland.
U53	21 February 1940	HMS *Gurkha* (1) off the coast of Orkney.
U55	30 January 1940	HMS *Whitshed*, *Fowey* (sloop) and aircraft south-west of the Scillies.
U63	26 February 1940	HMS *Escort*, *Imogen* and *Inglefield* of the south coast of Shetland.
U69	17 February 1943	HMS *Viscount* in the North Atlantic.
U70	8 March 1941	HMS *Wolverine* off the south coast of Iceland.

U-boat	Date of Attack	Details
U74	2 May 1942	HMS *Wishart*, *Wrestler* and aircraft off the coast of Cartagena.
U75	28 December 1941	HMS *Kipling* off the coast of Mersa Matruh.
U76	5 April 1941	HMS *Wolverine* with *Scarborough* (sloop) off the south coast of Iceland.
U79	23 December 1941	HMS *Hasty* and *Hotspur* off the coast of Tobruk.
U87	4 March 1943	HMCS *St Croix* and *Shediac* (frigate) south of Oporto.
U88	14 September 1942	HMS *Onslow* south of Spitsbergen.
U89	14 May 1943	HMS *Broadway* with *Biter* (escort carrier) and *Lagan* (frigate) and aircraft from *Biter* in mid-Atlantic.
U90	24 July 1942	HMCS *St Croix* off Newfoundland.
U93	15 January 1942	HMS *Hesperus* north of Madeira.
U99	17 March 1941	HMS *Walker* south of Iceland.
U100	17 March 1941	HMS *Vanoc* and *Walker* south of Iceland.
U110	9 May 1941	U110 was depth charged with such effect that she surfaced and surrendered and she was boarded, the crew transferred to HM ships and made safe for towing to a UK port but due to damage sustained during the attacks and possible sabotage by her crew she foundered in tow. HMS *Broadway*, *Bulldog* and *Aubretia* (corvette) were the attackers.
U131	17 December 1941	HMS *Blankney*, *Exmoor* and *Stanley* with aircraft from *Audacity* (escort carrier), *Stork* (sloop), and *Penstemon* (corvette) west of Madeira.
U138	16 June 1941	HMS *Faulknor*, *Fearless*, *Foresight*, *Forester* and *Foxhound* in the North Atlantic.
U147	2 June 1941	HMS *Wanderer* and *Periwinkle* (corvette) north-west of Ireland.
U162	3 September 1942	HMS *Pathfinder*, *Quentin* and *Vimy* off Trinidad.
U179	8 October 1942	HMS *Active* off Cape Town.
U186	12 May 1943	HMS *Hesperus* north of the Azores.
U187	4 February 1943	HMS *Beverley* and *Vimy* in the North Atlantic.
U191	23 April 1943	HMS *Hesperus* in the North Atlantic.
U201	17 February 1943	HMS *Fame* off Newfoundland.
U203	25 April 1943	HMS *Pathfinder* and aircraft from *Biter* (escort carrier) south of Greenland.
U205	17 February 1943	HMS *Paladin* and aircraft off Malta.
U207	11 September 1941	HMS *Leamington* and *Veteran* south of Greenland.
U223	30 March 1944	HMS *Blencathra*, *Hambledon*, *Laforey* and *Tumult* north of Palermo.
U229	22 September 1943	HMS *Keppel* south of Greenland.
U242	30 April 1945	HMS *Havelock* and *Hesperus* in the Western Approaches.
U274	23 October 1943	HMS *Duncan* and *Vidette* and aircraft south-west of Iceland.
U282	29 October 1943	HMS *Duncan* and *Vidette* and *Sunflower* (corvette) in mid-Atlantic.
U289	31 May 1944	HMS *Wanderer* and *Glenarm* (frigate) south-west of Ireland.
U306	31 October 1943	HMS *Whitehall* and *Geranium* (corvette) north of the Azores.
U314	30 January 1944	HMS *Meteor* and *Whitehall* south of Bear Island.
U325	30 April 1945	HMS *Havelock* and *Hesperus*, in the south Irish Sea.
U340	1 November 1943	HMS *Active*, *Witherington* and *Fleetwood* (sloop) and aircraft in the North Atlantic.
U344	24 August 1944	HMS *Keppel* and *Loch Dunvegan* (frigate) and *Mermaid* and *Peacock* (sloops) north of North Cape.
U353	16 October 1942	HMS *Fame* in mid-Atlantic.
U355	1 April 1944	HMS *Beagle* and aircraft from *Tracker* (escort carrier) south-west of Bear Island.
U357	26 December 1942	HMS *Hesperus* and *Vanessa* north-west of Ireland.
U360	2 April 1944	HMS *Keppel* north-west of Hammerfest.
U371	4 May 1944	HMS *Blankney* and USS *Pride* and *Campbell* (destroyer escorts) and FFS *Senegalais* (frigate) off the Algerian coast.

U-boat	Date of Attack	Details
U372	4 August 1942	HMS *Croome, Sikh, Tetcott* and *Zulu* and aircraft off Jaffa.
U381	19 May 1943	HMS *Duncan* and *Snowflake* (corvette) south of Greenland.
U390	5 July 1944	HMS *Wanderer* and *Tavy* (frigate) in Seine Bay.
U392	16 March 1944	HMS *Vanoc* and *Affleck* (frigate) and aircraft in the Straits of Gibraltar.
U394	2 September 1944	HMS *Keppel, Whitehall* and *Affleck* (frigate) and aircraft from *Vindex* (escort carrier) west of Harstadt.
U401	3 August 1941	HMS *St Albans, Wanderer* and *Hydrangea* (corvette) south-west of Ireland.
U407	19 September 1944	HMS *Garland, Terpsichore* and *Troubridge* south of Milos.
U409	12 July 1943	HMS *Inconstant* north of Algiers.
U411	15 November 1942	HMS *Wrestler* off Bone.
U413	20 August 1944	HMS *Forester, Vidette* and *Wensleydale* south of Brighton.
U434	18 December 1941	HMS *Blankney* and *Stanley* north of Madeira.
U443	23 February 1943	HMS *Bicester, Lamerton* and *Wheatland* off Algiers.
U444	11 March 1943	HMS *Harvester* and FFS *Aconit* (corvette) in mid-Atlantic.
U450	10 March 1944	HMS *Blankney, Blencathra, Brecon* and *Exmoor* off Anzio.
U453	21 May 1944	HMS *Liddesdale, Termagant* and *Tenacious* north of Sardinia.
U457	16 September 1942	HMS *Impulsive* north of Murmansk.
U458	22 August 1943	HMS *Easton* and RHN *Pindos* south of Pantellaria.
U472	4 March 1944	HMS *Onslow* and aircraft from *Chaser* (escort carrier) south of Bear Island.
U523	25 August 1943	HMS *Wanderer* and *Wallflower* (corvette) west of Vigo.
U531	6 June 1943	HMS *Oribi* and *Snowflake* (corvette) north of Newfoundland.
U559	30 October 1942	HMS *Hero, Hurworth, Dulverton, Pakenham* and *Petard* and aircraft north of Port Said.
U562	19 February 1943	HMS *Hursley* and *Isis* and aircraft north of Benghazi.
U568	28 May 1942	HMS *Eridge, Hero* and *Hurworth* north of Tobruk.
U581	2 February 1942	HMS *Westcott* south-west of the Azores.
U585	29 March 1942	HMS *Fury* off Vardo.
U587	27 March 1942	HMS *Aldenham, Grove, Leamington* and *Volunteer* in mid-Atlantic.
U589	12 September 1942	HMS *Faulknor* south-west of Spitsbergen.
U593	12 December 1943	HMS *Calpe* and USS *Wainwright* off Constantine.
U619	15 October 1942	HMS *Viscount* in mid-Atlantic.
U621	18 August 1944	HMCS *Chaudiere, Kootenay* and *Ottawa* off La Rochelle.
U651	30 June 1941	HMS *Malcolm* and *Scimitar* with *Violet, Speedwell* and *Arabis* (corvettes) south of Iceland.
U671	4 August 1944	HMS *Wensleydale* and *Stayner* (destroyer escort) off Brighton.
U678	6 July 1944	HMCS *Kootenay, Ottawa* and HMS *Statice* (corvette) off Brighton.
U713	24 February 1944	HMS *Keppel* north-west of Narvik.
U719	26 June 1944	HMS *Bulldog* in the North Atlantic.
U732	30 October 1943	HMS *Douglas* and *Imperialist* (trawler) off Tangiers.
U744	6 March 1944	HMS *Icarus* and HMCS *Chaudiere* and *Gatineau*, with *Kenilworth Castle* and HMCS *St Catherines* (frigates) also *Chilliwack* and *Fennel* (corvettes) in mid-Atlantic.
U761	24 February 1944	HMS *Anthony* and *Wishart* with aircraft off Tangiers.
U767	18 June 1944	HMS *Fame, Havelock* and *Inconstant* south-west of Guernsey.
U845	11 March 1944	HMS *Forester* and HMCS *St Laurent* with HMCS *Owen Sound* and *Swansea* (frigates) in mid-Atlantic.
U878	10 April 1945	HMS *Vanquisher* and *Tintagel Castle* (frigate) west of St Nazaire.
U971	24 June 1944	HMS *Eskimo* and HMCS *Haida* and aircraft off Ushant.
U984	20 August 1944	HMCS *Chaudiere, Kootenay* and *Ottawa* west of Brest.
U1195	6 April 1945	HMS *Watchman* south of Spithead.
U1199	21 January 1945	HMS *Icarus* and FFS *Mignonette* (corvette) off the Scillies.
U1274	16 April 1945	HMS *Viceroy* north of Newcastle.

Italian Submarines 1940–43

U-boat	Date of Attack	Details
Adua	30 September 1941	HMS *Gurkha* (2) and *Legion* in the western Mediterranean.
Alissandro Malaspina	21 September 1941	HMS *Vimy* in the North Atlantic.
Amiraglio Caracciolo	11 December 1941	HMS *Farndale* off Bardia.
Ascianghi	23 July 1943	HMS *Eclipse* and *Laforey* south of Sicily.
Anfitrite	6 March 1941	HMS *Greyhound* off Crete.
Asteria	17 February 1943	HMS *Easton* and *Wheatland* of Bougie.
Berillo	2 October 1940	HMS *Hasty* and *Havock* off Alexandria.
Cobalto	12 August 1942	HMS *Ithuriel* and *Pathfinder* off Rizerta.
Dagabur	12 August 1942	HMS *Wolverine* off Algiers.
Dessie	28 November 1942	HMS *Quentin* and *Quiberon* (RCN) north of Bone.
Durbo	18 October 1940	HMS *Firedrake*, *Wrestler* and aircraft east of Gibraltar.
Evangelista	22 June 1940	HMS *Kandahar*, *Kingston* and *Shoreham* (sloop) in the Red Sea.
Faa di Bruno	8 November 1940	HMS *Havelock* in the North Atlantic.
Galileo Ferraris	25 October 1941	HMS *Lamerton* and aircraft in the North Atlantic.
Glauco	27 May 1941	HMS *Wishart* west of Gibraltar.
Gondar	20 September 1940	HMS *Stuart* and aircraft off Alexandria.
Lafole	20 October 1940	HMS *Hotspur*, *Gallant* and *Griffin* east of Gibraltar.
Leonardo de Vinci	23 May 1943	HMS *Active* and *Ness* (frigate) north-east of the Azores.
Liuzzi	27 June 1940	HMS *Dainty* and *Ilex* off Crete.
Maggiori Baracca	8 September 1941	HMS *Croome*, north-east of the Azores.
Naide	14 December 1940	HMS *Hereward* and *Hyperion* off Bardia.
Narvalo	14 January 1943	HMS *Hursley*, *Pakenham* and aircraft south-east of Malta.
Neghelli	19 January 1941	HMS *Greyhound* in the eastern Mediterranean.
Nereide	13 July 1943	HMS *Echo* and *Ilex* in the Messina Straits.
Uebi Scebeli	29 June 1940	HMS *Dainty* and *Ilex* off Crete.
Varsciek	15 December 1942	HMS *Petard* and *Queen Olga* (Greek) south of Malta.

Japanese Submarines 1942–45

U-boat	Date of Attack	Details
160	17 January 1942	HMS *Jupiter*, 25 miles off Krakatoa.
127	12 February 1944	HMS *Paladin* and *Petard*, 60 miles from Adu Atoll.

APPENDIX 6

The 1-Ton Depth Charge Anti-Submarine Weapon Mark X

The 1-ton depth charge was developed in the Second World War to deal with the increasing depth to which U-boats could then submerge. The weapon (one only per destroyer) was discharged from a torpedo tube being of similar size to a 21in torpedo, which all destroyers carried, and would detonate at a depth of approximately 1,000ft. No records of the effectiveness of this weapon has been released, nor, despite contacting various naval museums and the MoD, does any photograph of this weapon appear to have been filed or released.

No attack was made on a U-boat using the Mark X weapon on its own; an attack was always by rocket, standard depth charge, Hedgehog or Squid, as was found when U570 was captured in the Second World War and evaluated after her refit trials.

APPENDIX 7

HM Destroyer Anti-aircraft Armament from L Class of WWI to O Class of WWII

PAGE	REMARKS AND COMMENTS
31, 32	L Class 1 – .303in MAXIM
32-36	M Class 2 – 1pdr or 1½pdr (later 2pdr)
38	Ex-Chilean 2 – 1pdr POM-POM (later 2pdr)
39	MARKSMAN leader 2 – 1pdr or 1½pdr (later 2pdr)
40	ANZAC Class as MARKSMAN
44	R Class as M Class
44, 45	Modified R 1 – 2 pdr
45	SABRE 1 – 2 pdr 1 – .303in MAXIM 4 – .303in LEWIS
49	VAMPIRE 2 – 2pdr later 1 – 3in HA
50	W Class as SABRE
54	BRUCE 1 – 3in HA 1 – .303mg
56	AMAZON 2 – 2pdr POM-POM
57	AMBUSCADE as AMAZON
57, 58	A Class 2 – 2pdr POM-POM 4 – .303 LEWIS
58	B Class , as A but with 1 – .303in VICKERS
59	C Class 1 – 3in HA, 2 – 2pdr POM-POM 4 – .303in LEWIS 1 – .303in VICKERS
61	D Class with 1 quad mtg 2 – 5in mg in lieu

PAGE	REMARKS AND COMMENTS
	of POM-POMS
62	E Class 2 – .5in quad mtg 4 – .303in LEWIS 1 – .303in MAXIM
63, 64	F Class as E Class
64, 65	G Class as E Class
65, 66	H Class as E Class
67, 68	TRIBAl Class 2 – 2pdr POM-POM 2 – .5in quad mtgs
69, 70	JAVELIN 2 – .5in quad 1 – 2pdr quad POM-POM 4 – .303in LEWIS
70	KELLY as JAVELIN
71	NAPIER 1 – 4in HA, then as MARKSMAN
71, 72	LAFOREY 1 – 4in HA 1 – 2pdr quad POM-POM 4 – 20mm OERLIKON 2 – .5in TWIN mtg 1 – .303in VICKERS
73	MARKSMAN 1 – 2pdr quad POM-POM 2 – .5in quad mg 2 – .303in LEWIS, thereafter 20mm OERLIKON were substituted for .5in mg
88	ORIBI as NAPIER

The above information is from *British Destroyers* by Edgar J. March, Seeley Service. The lighter weapons varied from ship to ship of all classes and types with vessels on particularly hazardous duties gaining from vessels on routine escort or refitting or in dry dock with vessels sunk in shallow water being dived on, to procure the above, such was the shortage in the early months of the Second World War.

Bibliography

A.J. Watts; *Japanese Warships of World War 2*; Ian Allan Ltd, 1968.

J.C. Taylor; *German Warships of World War 2*; Ian Allan Ltd, 1966.

H.M. Le Fleming; *Warships of World War 1, No. 3 Destroyers*; Ian Allan Ltd.

F.T. Jane; *Jane's Fighting Ships*; various editions, Sampson Low & Marston.

Peter Elliott; *Allied Escort Ships of World War II*; Macdonald & Janes, 1977.

Labayle Couhat; *Combat Fleets of the World 1976/77*; Arms & Armour Press.

R.V.B. Blackman; *The World's Warships 1955*; Macdonald.

H.T. Lenton; *British Fleet & Escort Destroyers 1, 1970*; Macdonald.

Navy Losses 1919; HMSO.

Mike Critchley; *British Warships and Auxiliaries 1979*; Maritime Books.

Alan Raven and John Roberts; *Ensign 6. War Built O to Z Class Destroyers*; Bivouac Books Ltd, 1975.

Captain T.D. Manning and Commander C.F. Walker; *British Warship Names 1959*; Putnam.

Captain S.W. Roskill; *Official History of the War at Sea*; HMSO.

Captain T.D. Manning; *The British Destroyer*; Putnam Books.

Edgar J. Marsh; *British Destroyers*; Seeley Services.

Captain T.D. Manning and Commander C.F. Williams; *British Warship Names*; Putnam Books.

J.J. Colledge; *Ships of the Royal Navy*; Greenhill Books.

Jurgan Rohwer; *Chronology of the War at Sea*; Greenhill Books.

OTHER SOURCES

Transactions of the Royal Institution of Naval Architects; various issues.

Combat Fleets of the World; various editions, United States Naval Institute.

Assistance from the Naval Historical Branch Admiralty, Whitehall (later Portsmouth).

Index of Ships' Names

Aerial view of the ship-breaking yard at Morecambe in 1921. The largest vessel is HMS *Diadem*, and behind it are German submarine U101 and HMS *Albion*. At the left-hand jetty are HMS *Mersey*, *Adventure*, *Kempenfelt* and *Peyton* in various stages of demolition. (Thos. W. Ward Ltd)

AIRCRAFT-CARRYING
SHIPS OF THE
ROYAL NAVY

MAURICE COCKER

With a Foreword by Admiral Sir Jeremy Black

Aircraft-Carrying Ships of the Royal Navy

978-0-7524-4633-2

Within ten years of man's first flight, the armies and navies of the world had seen the potential of the flying machine. This book looks at the ships of the Royal Navy which have carried and used aircraft since the first aircraft-carrier was built in 1912. It includes small lighters, battleships with runways on their turrets, and submarines.

Visit our website and discover thousands of other History Press books.
www.thehistorypress.co.uk